C000145879

Gallery Books
*Editor* Peter Fallon

FOUR SIDES FULL

Vona Groarke

# FOUR SIDES FULL

*A Personal Essay*

Gallery Books

*Four Sides Full*
is first published
simultaneously in paperback
and in a clothbound edition
on 6 October 2016.

## The Gallery Press

Loughcrew
Oldcastle
County Meath
Ireland

www.gallerypress.com

*All rights reserved. For permission
to reprint or broadcast this work,
write to The Gallery Press.*

© Vona Groarke 2016

ISBN 978 1 85235 684 2 *paperback*
     978 1 85235 685 9 *clothbound*

A CIP catalogue record for this book
is available from the British Library.

*Four Sides Full* receives financial assistance
from the Arts Council.

*for John McAuliffe*
*and for Helen O'Leary*

## Four Unpainted Frames

The child picks out suns and shoals, as she does.
Also a puzzle made of forbidding ghosts
and the rings her mother gave to the sea
the summer no one talks of any more.

The child knows it is no easy thing
to injure the frame or to fill it with water
or to make it spin like piano music
so all its glittery questions fall to the floor.

The frame has three yet unbroken ones
for the girl who dreams of love. Am I open
or closed? Am I quiet or silent? Where is
the end of me? But she does not care for riddles,

this child, so she sings to the back of the wall,
'I see you wherever you are'. Then she smiles
her not-for-the-life-of-me smile and gets up
on her tippy-toes, looks an answer in the eye.

The frame I choose for this day
is made of feathers and froth.

❖

As though someone carved
faintly decorous clouds
onto a pale grey sky:
this, my all-day canvas,
yet to be painted on.

❖

A rowdy sun like an offer of love
framed with the window's air quotes.

❖

The wall is in step with the picture rail.
God knows where this is headed.

❖

An afternoon evenly framed in bronze
like a skin colour given a name.

❖

And every promise ever made
was framed in a yellow frame.

❖

Gesso to neutralize the linen,
gilt to douse the grain.

❖

Run your eyes along the edge of me,
see where the world begins.

❖

Rooms with nothing on the walls:
who can tell what they're thinking?

❖

A picture slips infinitesimally.
A knot cosies up to thin air.

❖

The picture rail without pictures
has to grow old alone.

❖

Frame, mount, art:
yes, no, maybe?

❖

Me, ferreting for little poems
as the paintbrush does
for paint.

'I love you baby and I always will
ever since I put your picture in a frame.'
                    — Tom Waits, 'Picture in a Frame',
                                *Mule Variations*, 1999

A frame is a practical thing      (for protection)

A frame is functional      (for hanging)

A frame is powerful      (it adds value)

A frame is sly      (it flatters)

A frame is magic      (it transforms)

A frame makes itself clear.

A frame is a halo. A frame is a breach.
                    A frame is a no man's land.

A frame is an honour. A frame's an investment.
                    A frame's a proscenium arch.

A frame defines. A frame encloses.
                    A frame completes.

A frame declares that what's inside
                    is worthy of a frame.

The frame separates the artwork from the world around.
What's inside is art, what's outside is not — simple, isn't it?
As if around every experience there would be some kind of
transition, some way of saying, Prepare yourself, there will
be a crossing. So draw breath.

The image proposes an imagined world. The surrounding is
reality; it is where we are when we look at the image, the air
we breathe, the room we stand in, the wall we're allowed to

touch. The frame is the transition from imagined to real. That's a big responsibility when you think about it. No surprise then that the frame sometimes nudges towards excessive ornament, as if by being too much it can at least be sure of itself.

The mount confirms it. Wiped of noise and meaning, of business and intent, the mount is a meditative space. The mount will see you clear. You set aside your knots of living, shed your duties and concerns, you take a breath, dip your mind in its clean space, to emerge on the inner side of it. You have been prepared.

Can dimensions be conferred upon a meditative space? Call it an inch or two of potential, of virgin territory.

The gap between painting and frame: like when the orchestra finishes and there's a fraction of silence before applause kicks in.

A mount in the UK and Ireland, a mat in the US, it's a *passe-partout* in French, a 'goes everywhere', which is also the French term for a master or skeleton key. The defining characteristic of a passepartout is its lack of defining characteristics. Undecorated, undistinguished, the same mount can be used for all different kinds of art, it goes anywhere, which I suppose makes it a kind of skeleton key. Use the same mount with different art and different frames, there's still a seam of connection between how they look. It's not the full rhyme of matching frames, but a much quieter and slyer half-rhyme, a coincidence of sight, a filigree connection that the eye registers probably more fully than the mind. It's a kind of poor man's magic trick, like tracking the same consonants or vowels in different words, or the same shy huddle of sounds that runs like an undercurrent through a stanza or poem, pulling the thing together, unlocking a network of association, opening up possible meanings as a master key would a locked room.

The mount goes everywhere but is always contained by the

stronger claims of both artwork and frame. It's a means to an end, a transaction of sorts. It holds what contains it and what it contains in equilibrium.

Not every painting requires a mount; not every frame does either. Sometimes having a mount would be like listening to an opera duet with banjo accompaniment.

The verb 'to cleave' means to split or rend apart, and also to cling or hold fast. I like a word that holds its own between opposite meanings, that can look in two directions at once and settle right at the nexus of two competing and crossed lines.

Maybe every painting that wants to be beautiful should be framed in an ugly frame.

Memory works by slapping frames around the oddest things. Rarely understated, the frames, as I get older, seem to tend towards the gaudy, the baroque. Some are black lacquer, some are mirror glass. One or two are gold, burnished and ornate (there's no accounting for taste in the end, especially when it comes to the surface of metaphor). Some shatter on the slightest impact, some are studded with sharp tacks. A few have layers of black crêpe in front. With very little sense of what comes before or after, I can recall, as if it were the second when I began to write this sentence, single moments from forty years ago, and more. Here is me in a wicker cradle with a face looming in. Here is me in the back of a rowboat, baling out water with a baby-food can. Here is me in that hospital waiting room, playing with anagrams. I could go on. It's not like a film where scenes get played in sequence, so that the reason for this scene might be found in the last. It's more like a slide show without the projector. Unless I am the projector. Unless my body is.

There is a cigar box somewhere in a storage crate with three slides from the '60s inside. You know the ones, about two inches square with a thick card border in white, like a mini polaroid. If I hold them up to the light I will see my mother, my father, my brother and me in one of three locations: at the Alcock and Brown monument in Clifden, the Lia Fáil on the Hill of Tara or the Wellington Monument in Dublin. In two of them I will be wearing the red, blue and white candy-striped summer dress my Aunt Anna sent back from New York. (I loved that dress. As the youngest of six, clothes were valued more for being serviceable than for being smart, and that dress was probably the most colourful piece of clothes I'd ever had.) In the third we are all bundled up, my mother in a wool coat with big buttons that I swear I can *almost* smell the muffled brown of when I hold the slide up to the light. I remember nothing else of those three occasions; the slides are all there is. Year in, year out, they are in darkness. Ask me now, I'd scarcely know where I could put a hand to them. But sometime in the future, clearing a press or (God help me) maybe moving again, there will be the Café Crème box and I will open it and I will take out each slide, hold it up to a window and, sure as a director calling 'Action' or a race-gun going off, that single moment will light up, and my past, a few seconds of it framed as a slip of celluloid, and my dead parents and my young day will square up to my life.

*Life*: a word in which three of the letters seem to agree on a direction and the fourth has other ideas. It is practically silent, that 'e', a stowaway sheltering in the lea of the other ones. Three sides of a frame that occupy a vertical world, that see the world along the same more or less straight-up lines, and a fourth that curls round a protected space, as any life requires.

I was maybe six or seven, filling in the stretch between home from school and teatime, and I was playing outside. My mother was big on us playing outside, not *outside* in a Heathcliff and Cathy sort of way — untamed hills and folds of fields you could get lost in or encounter fairies or come back from, centuries having passed, a different child entirely.

No, outside had to be in view of the kitchen window or the back door or, at a push, outside the front door hitting a tennis ball against the gable wall, so she'd hear us within reach. I was probably larking with our old dog, Judy, or doing my best to annoy my brother but, either way, I'd have been lonely and bored, as I mostly remember being. I think I'd not yet learned to find in books the company I so badly wanted for real. I remember a lot of loitering, looking in windows of bedrooms, wondering if anything would be different seen from outside in, or if I'd catch anyone up to something. As if there were anyone to catch. But I did eke out a mystery all the same; not something happening inside rooms, but in the rooms themselves. The windows had something wrong with them: something didn't add up. From the inside the wall of the bedroom where I slept seemed to be mostly window. Likewise the room to the left of it, closest to the kitchen. These two big windows would surely have brushed almost against each other had there not been a dividing wall. Seen from the outside, however, there was a sizeable portion of wall separating them. I got my mother's measuring tape from the old Singer sewing machine. I tried to make them tally, the in-side and the out, but I couldn't. There was only one possible explanation: there had to be a secret windowless room sep-arating the two big windows, accounting for the stretch of unaccountable pebble-dash. I asked my mother what she kept in the secret room and when she told me there was no secret room I knew its contents had to be very important indeed. But what could be so secret that it had to be locked in a hidden room that my mother said didn't exist? I remem-ber at one stage being pretty sure that it must have been another child, a very quiet child, a better child than I; a child to be sheltered from the kind of sister who failed, every day, to come rescue her. These are the kinds of knots bored children tie up their lives in: complicated knots that double back on themselves and can't be undone, even with diagrams, even with the step-by-step account of how they came to be. The secret room with the better me. The secret room with another life so precious it had to be protected from me. And

I was only six or seven. Oh, you can be very sure I filled that room with the most fanciful content known to a midland youngest child who watched a lot of TV. I imagined it, based on the logic of the measuring tape, narrow, taller than it was wide, lit with exuberant chandeliers sometimes and, other times, blacker than the inside of my mouth in the small hours, fast asleep. I imagined it filled with precious jewels, and also filled with feathers or lightning, or with a strange and eerie greyness with no memory of colour or light. I imagined it where the witch lived when she wasn't underneath my bed, waiting to grab my ankles. I imagined it New York, where my mother and her stories came from. It was a lab where gold was made by a man in a white coat who could not speak. And it was where all my new friends were waiting for me, ready to jump out and call, 'Surprise!'.

Later on when I first walked into an art gallery, in Dublin, I saw in all those high gilt frames the inside of that room. And it was like nothing I'd imagined. And it was like it all.

When you google-image a painting it almost always shows without a frame. As though all paintings could be equal, or be made to be. It's very disconcerting, like catching a female relative in some state of undress. They tend to look a little sorry for themselves, a small bit abashed.

'The four sides of a frame are among the most important parts of a picture. A painting or a drawing included in a given space ought, therefore, to be in perfect harmony with the frame . . . according to the dimensions of the room in which it is to be hung.'
— Henri Matisse[i]

Here are styles of ornament commonly used in frames:
*Lamb's tongue, guilloche, egg and dart, crocket, palmette, ogee, gesso, mortise and tenon, acanthus, raking knull, ribbon and stick, sgraffito, gadroon, rocaille.*
— Here are words that have been carved to gilded ornament. Part armour, part fancy dress, the point of the frame is

to protect and to enhance. But no armour is made from skin, whereas some frames are made from the same wood as the painted panel. In early Byzantine icons, for example, the frame is carved from the same panel as the painting, with the painted place recessed in the centre of the piece. It's a difference of depth, with the frame concerned more with the third dimension than with width or height. I wish I could do that with a poem, surround it in a depth of space. Depth could be very useful in the framing of a poem.

Inside is the poem. Outside is not. The poem's white space is a framing device. But white space is not a fashioned thing: it is negative space. The un-poem.

'Yes, I remember Adlestrop.'[ii] The Edward Thomas poem opens at a slant: something has been said or thought, and the first line is the response. What is it answering? Is there a question ('Do you remember Adlestrop?' perhaps)? From its first breath the poem is in league with another that is not heard. There is context, a world elsewhere, against which the poem is set, much as a framed picture is positioned on a wall.

That wall is our world, where we live and from where we must make a journey if we are to step over the threshold of the unheard that introduces this poem. The quietness of the poem is what we step into with relief, trailing our ever-so-busy lives, asking for a minute's peace so we can set them down like so many shopping bags and simply draw our breath. The poem stills us, just as the moment stilled Edward Thomas back on that heated late June afternoon, just as the moment was then settled by him in the four straight, hinged stanzas of the poem. The poem invites us into its carriage, there to sit and listen not only to its birdsong, but to the sweet machine of the well made poem progressing stealthily. The poem re-enacts its moment of composition: we are there, immediately, sat on that express train. That may well be me or you who has just cleared his throat.

But we must be quiet now: the poem hushes its surround-sound to listen for those birds. It begins with unheard words and finishes in silence, as all poems do, the clatter of that blackbird and his companions fading as the train pulls out, and as the poem fades out into silent, white space and, beyond it, into busy hands that hold the book and lives that are so noisy they beg for a moment's silence now, for a moment's respite. This poem is first framed by silence, and then it is framed by noise.

We can stand in front of this framed silence and, if the frame is strong enough to take the weight, we can enter it. Perhaps every poem wants to position itself inside some frame or another; perhaps this is why it is a poem and not a piece of prose with its altogether looser arrangement with the white space of the page. Perhaps every well made poem is capable of saying to us, This is a full world. And it is up to us to measure the truth of it against the truth of our elsewhere lives.

If no white space cushioned the poem its language would have to brush up against the language of the world. The world where language buys sausages and fills insurance forms. Where it writes rejections and makes empty promises. Where it speaks in parliaments and fudges truth and sells cosmetic surgery and guns. And if there were no white space to mark it off, how would we know the difference? They are only little words. Even the innocent amongst them look like repeat offenders, like the lying sort.

'Don't play what's there,' Miles Davis said, 'play what's not there.'[iii] Play the void. Play the white space. Play outside the frame.

If only there were ways of framing off the worst of our lives. Of containing it. Forbidding it to leak into the rest of our well-lived days.

Which sounds as if a frame is a high wall, keeping what's inside captive, at a safe distance. But a frame is not a wall: it cannot be. The point of a frame is that it is not-wall. It is the un-wall.

One popular contemporary frame for oils: plain, thin white wood. This is a frame that says, like the elderly aunt at a party, 'Oh, don't mind me, I'm fine here by myself. You go and enjoy yourselves.' But then, because we are (mostly) kind, we end up sitting with the aunt, listening to a story about an encounter with a watermelon or how rude most drivers are. Riveting it may not be but it has a compulsive tedium that begs to be seen through. That white frame pretends to be part of the wall, to blend into the background, literally. And because it really isn't part of the wall (it's made of different material, and has a different plane and angles, not to mention its own purpose), the pretence is fascinating. It's a ploy of realism and, like all realism, I suspect, is intensely aware of its own artifice. And, like most emphasized humility, it has something of the decoy about it. Something inherently sly.

Vincent van Gogh to his brother Theo: 'I can only finish in a frame.'[iv]

My daughter, a fine art student, is learning about oils. First, they are taught to stretch a canvas, walking in a group round to the wood shop where they each buy matched-up lengths. These they use to make a frame, a stretcher, onto which they will tack the canvas before applying paint. She invites me to her studio on the top floor of the art college with a view of church spires across the river and a window through which the wind wheedles on even this spry day. She turns the canvas round to show me the frame she made. Her first, and yet she has got it true, lined up and confident, shipshape angles with no daylight bothering the joints.

This is the other frame that every painting keeps to itself, the frame the outer frame adheres to, all the way round; the bone-*hús*, the skeleton, the support — the simple frame that must hold true if the painting is to last. Of course it must hold its edges right and cannot be carved or embellished. But does anyone colour this frame, I wonder, or paint their initials on it, or run their hands along the grain and name the wood for the tree? This frame is primarily purposeful, and yet may it not have a kind of beauty that is not to do with ornament, but with timbre and serviceable strength? I cherish the notion that there can be beauty even where there is not; that a certain kind of pure function redefines how beauty works. This inner frame keeps the outer one honest: I think of it as its conscience, its straight-talking, no-claptrap take on the utility to ornament ratio. As such it's a corrective and a balancing act, pure form set against excess. Having nothing much to do with beauty, it cleaves aesthetic sense. It is fact to the outer frame's fiction, being steadfast and in earnest and committed, without distraction, to its use.

What is the beautiful human act? It can hardly be the act of being beautiful and yet that seems to pass, more than it should, as enough. In theory selflessness and kindness are received, not as aesthetic acts, but as nonetheless beautiful. (Once, drunk, I gave a homeless man twenty dollars. He told me I was a beautiful woman and I chose to believe he was right.) We comfort ourselves that, despite appearances, we may have beauty in us. We talk about the beauty of old people and we understand that we mean a very different kind of beauty from that of the virile young. We mean, I suppose, moral beauty: fortitude, calm, kindness and grace. It's a helpful thought, a comforting thought, that in my self of selves (that no one can see and therefore disprove) there may be yet a kind of beauty to distinguish me. We are all on the side of the angels so, the beautiful angels who weigh appearance against action and reward the latter, if it is useful and selfless and does its job without clamour or contrivance, but efficiently and true.

I would like to say I have lived my life with the good sense and application of an inner frame, but vanity will not allow me. There is too much ornament about me, geegaws, pictures on walls and a certain pair of suede yellow boots — too much money spent over the years on what has yet to prove itself as indispensable. I suppose like most people I live some-where between the fanciful and the serviceable. I strive for beauty and aesthetic worth, but have learned over decades to look for it beyond my prosaic frame. Art, music, writing, the world in all its wounded glory, and the way people find of being beautiful, one way or another — they each of them keep me looking outward, through the membrane of raw canvas, all potential; to the buttress of raw wood supporting itself; to the tacks and nails, more character than dash, and out the other side to colour and scheme and composition, to arrive finally at a beyond world that knows how to map the passage, and how to see it through.

The inner frame may be my private self, that never sees daylight and is unavailable to the world, that allows itself to be hidden to keep inviolable and safe. Every artist learns how best to protect this self because, without it, the impulse to make art solidifies so nothing comes of it. It's a taskmaster, this private self, so bossy and so absolute with its rules and instructions, its impossible, unreadable manual that must be intuited and then committed to memory and consulted at every turn. It cannot, it stipulates, be traded for intimacy or recorded in minutes or memoranda, or pinned down in manifestos, or sold in the marketplace. Much gets sacrificed so this essential self can hold its ground. Marriages, friendships, relationships, perfectly practicable jobs: the wrong question is asked (sometimes in innocence), or a claim is staked. Sometimes it's a form that needs filling, or a box that needs ticking, or a door opened when it needs to stay shut, or a gift that requires the wrong kind of thanks, or a conversation shouldered into places it has no right to go. Sometimes it's a dim-witted review, a claim by someone to know more, much more, than they have any business doing, and sometimes it's a word when silence would have suited better, or silence when a word was needed, impossible to call. Who on earth could get it right? It's a minefield. And yet squander this privacy on too many dinners or box sets or pillow talk, then see how it slips away, water through sand, nothing to show for its presence and no made mark.

An unstretched canvas can't sustain itself. Though I am awkward and oddly angled, hard to please, sharp-tongued and arch, these are, I believe it, self-protective mechanisms, practised over years and years, polished and refined. My public self, such as it is, is a frame of my designing. But the other frame, that hidden frame, is not for fashioning or trimming. Ornery and querulous, it makes itself available in only the exact right kind of silence and solitude. And, of course, it hates them both equally but at least I can say it hates them closely and it hates them carefully.

The metaphor is writing me into an artwork, which is silly, of course.

This is how I understand it. Another person will understand it differently, will find in communion a sustenance that confirms their creative selves. But my metaphor can't accommodate that: the inner frame can't be required to rearrange itself, not for anyone or any circumstance, unless the artwork needs to be dismantled and a fresh start made. I can't reinvent myself, I have materials to work with and I have spent the past twenty-five years of a writing life getting to grips with how they work and what's to be done with them. My past, my personality, my ethos, my bent: I write my poems along their edges and, by their untreated surfaces, feel a way to keep to myself.

'In this mortal frame of mine which is made of a hundred bones and nine orifices there is something, and this something is called a wind-swept spirit for lack of a better name, for it is much like a thin drapery that is torn and swept away at the slightest stir of the wind. This something in me took to writing poetry years ago, merely to amuse itself at first, but finally making it its lifelong business.'
— Matsuo Bashō, *The Narrow Road to the Deep North and Other Travel Sketches*

Patrick Kavanagh also said something of the kind: 'I dabbled in verse and it became my life.' Most poets would recognize the truth of it: who, for heaven's sake, would set out to be a poet? A poet is something you end up being because it may well be the only way you find to make sense of this life. Every good poem acknowledges its mortal frame, its hundred bones and nine orifices (call it form), but it also knows part of its work is to seek out the better name for that wind-swept spirit. The search will take it into darkness, surely, from which it may never return. I imagine a space filled with all the unresolved or unfinished poems there ever were. I imagine it a noisy place, buzzing with phrases that spill themselves over and over again, and no sense to be made of them now. As I leave I flick off the light, and the bits and bobs of poems that never did come right fall quiet the way fledglings do at nightfall when darkness releases them.

The inner frame of a painting does its work in darkness, covered in on all sides, as it tends to be, by encompassing canvas. This is one of many darknesses a framed painting frames. Here is another: the panel set off by the back of the frame, between painting and wall, where a three-dimensional darkness spills into the corners and edges to occupy itself.

Imagine any gallery space, all those boxed-in darknesses behind the paintings on show. Who will dust them or air them out? It bothers me to think of darkness as a fixed entity: regardless of whatever light might do to these ceilings, floors and walls, this darkness remains unperturbed. It never gets to let down its guard, to soften or lighten up. How can it bear its own weight? How are the paintings themselves not riddled with the backlog of darkness each of them maintains?

It makes a sequence: behind darkness, art; and before it, on the other side, as far from darkness (or at least, this specific darkness) as is possible, us. But not me: I'm there with my light metre and measuring tape, trying to gauge the depth and breadth, the heft and density of each dark slab. Like assigning twenty-one grams to the weight of the soul (as Dr Duncan MacDougall did) I play a daft numbers game.

All these panels of darkness mirroring each other in their separate cells: it bothers me and it comforts me too that darkness might conduct itself along predictable lines, for contrast and for company, and because it has no choice.

In his 'Metaphysical Still Life' series Morandi often paints a frame inside the picture. Sometimes empty, sometimes containing objects, sometimes deliberately not containing the objects that sit on top of it or partially obscure it from the front, these frames are very aware of their physicality, the shadows thrown by their sides, inside and out. The still lifes we might think of as typical Morandi, those vases and bottles and jugs, will typically have the plainest of plain frames. Those frames have something very simple to say, but the frames of the 'Metaphysical Still Lifes' have something to say that is less than simple. What they contain, ultimately, are questions and contradictions. They turn the inside out and rearrange natural order. Their emptiness is anything but: with their impossible dimensions and magical spaces, which everything and nothing might occupy, these frames seem like projections or symbols or signifiers of some sort, oddly angled between realism and the opposite of it, which sometimes looks like surrealism. Strange to be thinking about real or unreal frames inside paintings that are only as real as one believes them to be. Layers upon layers. Frames within frames. What is really there?

There is the historic past of a painting, its history and provenance. And then there is the timeline of your engagement with it. Which sometimes is a literal one (I saw the show reviewed in a newspaper, I bought an admission ticket, I travelled to the gallery, I went through three other rooms before . . . ) and sometimes is not. Here is another narrative that doesn't run along parallel lines with the way time does: 'I approached the painting from the left, I stood bang in front of it, I took two steps back, I walked on to the right.' Call it a spatial narrative. This is the one mediated, orchestrated by the picture frame. First one enters its claimed space, then one proceeds to the space of the painting, and then one passes out of this, over the physical space of the picture frame once again. It is a threshold, a portal: you cannot access the painting without crossing the frame. And, like every bouncer, the frame needs, once in a while, to flex a little muscle, to crowd your sight line, bear down a little, keep you in your place.

25

*Your place.* Time was, frames were made of wood from locally growing trees. You could tell, to a fair extent, the geographic profile of a frame from the wood used. Then more possibilities entered the frame as mahogany and ebony and other expensive woods were imported. The use of exotic wood in a frame indicated wealth and prestige: frames became status symbols, and social prestige and net worth was the kind of information seventeenth-century Dutch portraits, for example, were often interested in conveying about their subjects. Frames became committed to having as much to say about money as about aesthetics or art. Sometimes that information was also relayed by the artwork, but not always: a portrait suggests a person with resources to commission one, sure, but a still life isn't often or always arranged around money. So the frame picked up the slack. A frame could be like an ermine collar on a good overcoat, converting the serviceable into something also expensively decorative. Its business was not always the obvious business: it had several kinds of truth to tell, and it didn't always tell them equally.

But, oh, those seventeenth-century Dutch frames have so much beauty in them. Ebony makes for a very solemn, self-aware, no-nonsense kind of frame. Except, imagine it in candlelight: imagine the play on polished black, what the sheen and drama of it would do for the painting inside. I wonder if the use of so much black in the paintings of Rembrandt, for example, was something to do with the frame that would likely be chosen to contain it. How one black might answer to another. How a dull black oil might talk back to the polished wood surround. How vivid that conversation might be, how it could fill a room.

A wooden frame answers to other uses of wood within a room. Chairs and tables, window slats, doors and floorboards, all the rest of it. Frames too are a kind of furniture, functional and ornamental. Because if they weren't we'd never consider the context of the room when we choose a frame, we'd think only of what will be placed within. But that's not how it works. We choose wood that thinks about the grain and timbre of the table it overlooks. We paint that wood with something else in mind, the fleck of tweed in the curtain to the left, the grey of the sofa. As though nothing really stands alone. As though anything could.

The frame is framed by the room it is in. And by the doorway through which we enter the room, and by the rooms to any side of it and the rooms beyond those. And by the gallery building, and by what's outside it, a park, maybe, and a city and the country and a world. Which also holds other cities, other galleries, other rooms and other frames. It's all a matter of perspective: it depends on where you stand.

Football jerseys, certificates, letters, photographs, milk teeth, locks of hair, mirrors, coins, butterflies, dried flowers, tiles, gold records, admission tickets, receipts, samplers, clocks, anything made by one's children, flags and pennants, mottoes, pens, coats of arms, beer mats, addressed envelopes, scorecards, report cards, greeting cards, holy relics, lace, masks, autographs, spyholes, keys, jewellery, record sleeves, hospital tags, paper napkins — All these I have seen mounted in frames. Once, in a framer's in Dundalk, I waited my turn while the man in front explained exactly how he wanted the tricolour, black beret and leather gloves of a dead IRA man mounted. 'Yes, sir,' said the framer, a little urgently, and I'm sure, in his position, I'd have said exactly the same.

Though stripped of all of his Tour de France titles his seven yellow jerseys are all behind glass in Lance Armstrong's home. They no longer relate to a victory, only to a story. The line of significance has been thwarted, warped. What do the jerseys now signify? From what are they being protected? If Armstrong still believes he was victimized does he take comfort in his jerseys being framed?

*To be framed*: to be set up, to be made to look guilty of a crime one didn't commit.

*You've Been Framed*: a television programme featuring home footage of slapstick misadventures of humans and their pets. I'm never sure about the title: does it imply that the people featured have been set up, that these apparently spontaneous gaffes are scripted and choreographed? Or does it mean that something that happens in life is marked out by the act of being filmed, that it has a frame conferred upon it, a frame of time (these seven seconds, that minute-and-a-half)? I never quite believe in that frame. I can't help but project to either side of it: I imagine the kid with the skateboard with a mind of its own, or with the puppy that barks in time to Judy Garland, or the exploding paddling pool, going into school next day, how he'll likely be greeted with a mix of envy and derision. How those few seconds might come to define that day, that week, that year. How in years to come that same kid might remember a time in his life as the time he was on *You've Been Framed*, how those few seconds might scroll out to cover a swipe of time, a whole swathe of his life.

'The frame is the pimp of the painting.'
— Edgar Degas.[v]

In the 1740s a head and shoulder portrait by English pastellist, William Hoare, would have set you back five guineas. Framed and glazed the same portrait would cost an additional sixty percent — eight guineas.[vi] Either that's a painter who undervalued his art or a framer who overvalued his. Or maybe Mr Hoare made his own frames, in which case he was a canny man.

In 1804 art dealer William Buchanan wrote to his agent, 'It is wonderful how much better pictures sell by being in handsome, rich, deep frames.'[vii] Fine for the dealer, fine for the framer, not so good for the artist. But it's never so bad that it might not be worse. By 1828 Thomas Uwins, something of a painter *maudit* despite his professional success — he held a number of high profile positions, including Keeper of the National Gallery — was claiming, 'I believe frames pay more than pictures.'[viii] But he stayed at the painting anyway, until his death in 1857, though who cares now for the collected art of Thomas Uwins and his many glanced-over portraits or his many expensive frames?

Owing to religious persecution in the mid-eighteenth century, Protestant Huguenots fled France for England, bringing their crafts and the tools of their trades, including framemaking, with them. Their styles and fashions were new to England, more sculptural and more lavish: they became all the rage. Paul Petit made frames for Frederick, Prince of Wales. Isaac Gosset became Framemaker to the King. Framemaking is labour intensive and in the eighteenth century, pre-moulding it needed a lot of space. In 1763 William Linnell's workshops occupied three floors at No. 28 Berkeley Square, 'comprising a showroom, office, glass room and joinery shop on the ground floor, cabinet making and upholstery apparently on the first floor and the carving and gilding shops at the top of the building.'[ix] Framemaking was a fiddly business involving a number of different processes including joinery, carving, whitening, gold sizing, gilding and finishing. Different spaces had different requirements: 'Gilding, for example, needed a clean atmosphere in which sawdust from the joinery department would not settle on the gold size, and an even temperature, since the sizing and gilding process could be adversely affected by extremes of heat or cold.'[x]

Frames were an expensive business. In 1769 Gainsborough's whole-length portrait of Garrick was framed at a cost of £74 4s compared with the £63 the artist had been paid. In 1677 Mary Beale charged £1, £1 10s or £2 for a thirty by twenty-five inch frame, depending on the style, although it was possible to buy a plain black frame with a gold edge for a measly 16s. Fast forward to the 1820s and your rococo frame is likely to set you back five or six guineas. In 1918 William Orpen was using six-inch wide Whistler frames finished in white enamel, priced at £5 each. And in the 1930s simple frames of twenty-four by twenty inches cost £2, £2 10s and £3 10s.[xi] Despite the hand-carved gilded peaks and the plain, black troughs, between 1677 and the 1930s, frame prices had barely doubled. Can the same be said of any other craft, I wonder? Even poetry?

A parable, of sorts.

Imagine you have a portrait of King Charles I hanging in your stately halls. You are standing in front of it one morning in the mid-seventeenth century wondering what to do. The portrait was not cheap, the cost of it and its carved, gilded frame amounted to considerable outlay at the time, but the portrait was not entirely commissioned for its own sake. It was a statement of loyalty and allegiance. 'Look,' said the portrait, 'my owner has spent a small fortune on me and has hung me in the most prominent position in the house. Now what does that tell you?' But it is January 30th, 1649, and news has arrived that the king has been executed this morning at Whitehall. The kind of statement the painting now makes is, at best, controversial; at worst, dangerous. It is no longer just a painting (was it ever?): it is a liability. But it is an expensive liability, burning it would seem a shame, although perhaps a usefully public shame, in these dangerous days. Perhaps it could be sold abroad and some of the value recouped? And so the portrait is removed and a courier found to carry it to more comfortably royalist walls in France. Of course the courier cannot be expected to bear the burden of the frame, and so the portrait is relieved of its frame as the king's body was of his head. Now it is only a frame in a storeroom, propped up against a dusty, whitewashed wall. But someone, it occurs to you, might ask in a threatening voice what image the frame used to house. And so another painting is ordered, this time a landscape, trees and hills, a river signifying nothing from one edge to the other. The landscape is commissioned to fit the frame and is hung in all its pretty innocence where the king used to preside.

Sometimes the painting has the best lines; sometimes it's the frame.

In 1789, in revolutionary France, the Republican government

abolished the guild system and closed the associated work-shops. The framing business was gutted. Given that the leaders were not averse to sitting for portraits, presumably they had nothing against art. But the guilds were an organized net-work, and organized networks pose a threat to fledgling and precarious governments. Paris, to that point market leader in ornate frames, became a backwater. The fashion flipped towards other geographies, other styles. It's not known what became of the frames being made inside the workshops when they were peremptorily (as everything was in those heady days) shut. Tinder? Export? Black market trade? Imagine all that stockpiled gilt, those umpteen, unfilled frames.

After the Revolution framing picked up much where it left off. Antiquity was an abiding fashion and the same orna-mental and symbolic motifs maintained. How can this be? After the rampant violence of the Revolution, the class purges and the bloody reprisals, after so much tumultuous chaos, it seems extraordinary that something, anything, would revert to its pre-revolutionary state, as if nothing much had changed.

Napoleon had a fetish for classicism: presumably he thought it lent him a more Caesarean edge. His Egyptian campaigns had introduced him to decorative motifs such as palmettes and papyrus forms, and his picture frame of choice, the Empire Frame, featured these as plaster-cast ornaments on austere, rather sharp moulding. Imagine him having a favourite type of picture frame! Imagine him taking the time to decide that almost every painting in the Louvre should be reset in this Empire Frame! Is this what happens to generals when their wars are done and dusted and they lie safely in too solid beds? Do the fiercest soldiers retire to opinions on décor?

In 1851, at the height of Imperialist expansion, Prince Albert decided that all the paintings in Buckingham Palace should be rehoused in matching frames. Coincidence? Perhaps.

Burn a gilt frame, you're left with the gilt: it is the wood only that burns. In France during World War II, museums, where they could, bought frames to preserve them from the Germans who burnt them to recover the gilt to augment their war coffers.

During the Siege of Leningrad — when German troops surrounded the city, when over a million people died (mainly of starvation and related diseases), when people fell down dead crossing the street, when families swopped pets so as not to have to eat their own, when the city closed its ears to rumours of cannibalism — a group of Siberian cadets who had helped evacuate the museum's valuable French furniture was given a guided tour of the Hermitage. Pavel Gubchevsky, longtime tour guide at the museum, brought them around, room by room, but what they saw was not the paintings but the frames in which the paintings had hung before the war, now safely stored elsewhere. Gubchevsky described what had been in the frames as if the paintings were still there. 'That was the most curious excursion in my life,' he recalled, '. . . Even the empty frames left an impression.'[xii] Seventy-five years on from then I visit. I see a photograph of one of those rooms, frame after empty frame maintaining its space; something bereft about them all, but something defiant too. A room of vigilant, empty frames is not a defeated room. It promises to come back to life and it seems to be listening for the signal to do so. It forgets nothing, holds its past intact. Biding time, it waits and waits. And then recovers itself.

On April 26th, 1974, Rose Dugdale knocked at the front door of Russborough House pretending to be French and to be in need of help for her broken-down car. When the door was opened three masked and armed men stormed in, tied up the elderly owners of the house, the Beits, and then followed Ms Dugdale around the house while she selected which paintings would be stolen, including two by Gainsborough, three by Rubens, a Goya and a Vermeer. They cut nineteen paintings from their frames with a screwdriver and made off in a Ford

Cortina. On May 4th Gardaí found the full stash in the boot of the car outside a rented cottage at Glandore, County Cork.

In August 2010 thieves targeting Van Gogh's 'Poppy Flowers' in the Mahmoud Khalil Museum in Egypt dragged a couch under it and cut the painting from its frame with boxcutters.

St Patrick's Day, 1990. Two men in police uniforms wearing fake moustaches gained access to the Isabella Gardener Museum in Boston by claiming they were investigating a disturbance. In the next ninety minutes over a dozen paintings worth over £300 million, including a Rembrandt, a Vermeer and a Manet, were cut from their frames and removed from the building. No one has ever been charged with the theft and the paintings are still missing.

The preferred heist method of most art thieves is to cut the painting from the frame. That way it's more easily concealed and transported in pillowcases or poster tubes, or rolled up in black bin bags. Of course you're damaging the painting, leaving seams of it behind, but it's quickly managed and what you're left with has precious little weight in it, nothing to slow you down.

I can't help but think of all those left-behind frames clinging to their millimetres of frayed-edge canvas, still the same frames they were the day before, and yet diminished, entirely bereft. Like a couple going separate ways, one to stay in the family home and keep guard over an absence, the other to light out for the world, for better or for worse.

'Art consists of limitation. The most beautiful part of every picture is in the frame.'
— G K Chesterton[xiii]

Sometimes artists choose the frame: more often they do not. It's hard to know if you're looking at an original choice, one the artist made. Very few pictures are now seen in their original frames: the frame is how history enters the painting, how its timeline expands. The frame is how curators and patrons and architects elbow their way into artistic practice and, by applying taste and aesthetic choices, how they frame the narrative and assert an influence. They say to the painting, Sit up when I tell you. Speak when you're spoken to.

In the 1980s the Guggenheim Museum in New York had the period frames removed from paintings and showed them 'naked'. The argument was that a picture ought to stand by itself and that the frame interfered with the integrity of the painting. That must have been fascinating, like walking into a dressing room, or into an artist's studio. A frame declares an artwork finished. Without frames I wonder if those paintings looked still in development, still in production, still liable to change?

Perhaps they loaned what had been removed to the Chicago Art Institute for its 1986 exhibition of frames. Just frames. That must have been a strange experience, conceptual and yet doggedly physical, with all that material and form. I imagine it would be like a conversation in different languages, everyone speaking at right angles, a little too loudly, and with very little of substance to anchor it. It would sound like a Philip Glass concerto, all surface and little traction. A little insubstantial, maybe, but conceptually pretty, and wondrous glittery in light.

Another exhibition that has no truck with frames: Lascaux with its horses and bulls. There's something almost hallucinogenic about the way the eye ranges so giddily over the cave paintings without the pauses required by frames. And because they don't have frames the effect is of a total world, a complete and holistic visual experience that is intensely, sublimely, felt. The paintings exist out of time, thousands of years annihilated by their immediacy. How odd that the moving images they evoke break themselves down into frames per second. These images are not even frames per millennium; they are frameless in an abstract time that we can barely slap numbers or dates on, that has a time-busting power in it, that seems to expand consciousness more readily than it sections it off.

34

Theodore Rousseau's 'Forest of Fontainebleau' (1849) is a pretty landscape composed around a central space into which the forest leans on either side and daylight comes to life. There are cows by a pond. There is transformative golden light. A perfect promise is made. The back of the painting is another story, a more realist one, perhaps. There's a stamp on the rear of the canvas from an art supply shop, and labels of various exhibitions in which the painting has been shown. On the frame is a dealer's label, stuck there like a brand. The back of the painting and frame tells a story of nuts and bolts, of money and materials, of the ways in which the painting turns its back on perfected landscape, to face commerce and compromise; money and power; grub and making do. It's a better story, really, if one likes to find in art a chime with what's familiar in life. If I curated that gallery I'd display 'Forest of Fontainebleau' every second day with the oils turned to the wall.

Victorian galleries liked their wall space firmly covered up. Think *Mr Turner*, every inch of wallpaper between wainscot and coving jam-packed with art. Paintings crammed in, cheek by jowl, like crowd scenes in a London film, all bustle and impassivity. The frames of these paintings stop them from bumping up against each other. They mark the extent of one painting, the beginning of another. They're essentially captions reading 'Stop' / 'Go'; 'Walk' / 'Don't Walk'. Exhausting really, these frames with their imperatives. No wonder they are gilded loudly, being obliged to shout so much.

In the way book collectors used to have their books bound as a collection in identical bindings, fashionable nineteenth-century art collectors had their purchases mounted in identical frames. House style. Didn't matter if the painting was a delicate portrait or a grand-scale biblical theme. Same frame, different size. This changed how frames were manufactured: if you need a hundred identical frames, let's say, wouldn't you as a framer devise a way to standardize production?

In the late eighteenth century Thomas Jackson, working in his London workshop, developed a new type of framing material, composition ornament, known now as 'compo'. This was a malleable resin, easily pressed into moulds and good at holding its shape. It offered a cheap alternative to carving, being, in a sense, mass-producible: the moulds could be re-used, of course, and the resin was the product of a combination of inexpensive materials such as turpentine, linseed oil, glycerine, whiting, rosin and pearl glue. Compo changed the trade. Instead of hand-carving ornament, it could now be moulded and glued into place. The uniqueness of each carved frame came at a high price: in contrast, once gilded in sharp or burnished gold, compo looked plenty fancy and expensive at a fraction of the price. And, since ornament was cheaply and easily managed with it, ornament became commonplace. By 1864 Charles Eastlake, later the Keeper of the National Gallery, complained in *Cornhill Magazine* that 'rococo scrolls and tortuous nonentities . . . which pretend to be the result of so much labour are chopped by the dozen out of the meanest material'.[xiv] Gilt ornament, in other words, was no longer a signifier of the owner's wealth or status. All kinds of frames were uniformly gilded in a heavy-handed gold. The frames were chunky, oppressive and bossy. Something had to give.

In her *Lectures in America* Gertrude Stein writes: 'The Louvre at first was only gold frames to me gold frames which were rather glorious, and looking out of the window of the Louvre with the gold frames being all gold behind within was very glorious . . . somehow there with the gold frames and all, there was an elegance about it all, that did not please me, but that I could not refuse, and in a way it destroyed paintings for me.'[xv]

The Pre-Raphaelites played framing for a high stakes game. Specially commissioned for a particular painting, the Pre-Raphaelite frame tends to complete the painting with literary quote and allusion, and decorative Gothic motifs. These frames, opulent and rather self-involved, seem to see themselves as the ultimate context for the art within. A frame like that has a certain kind of hauteur: it gets along with its wall as a Victorian wife of means gets along with her chambermaid.

But that wasn't the only story, as one might expect of a society much given to the cover-up. Certain Pre-Raphaelites favoured a curious hinged glass frame that did away with the need for varnish when exhibiting oils.

The frame had a latch you pulled towards you, like an old-fashioned chute, to open the space inside. You simply lifted the painting in and out. This was a serviceable and recyclable frame, as long as you kept within its dimensions. How would that work? You have a canvas of exactly the right size to fit the frame stretched and ready for painting. Your last painting was, let's say, a Shakespeare scene. This one will have to be the same size. What will you paint? Already you have a vision of how the finished painting will be presented, of how the packaging looks. It's a little like writing poems in form: you know it needs to be fourteen lines, with a pre-determined rhyme scheme. Or thirty-nine lines with six end words repeated in a pattern, just so. So far it's a numbers game, as the canvas dimensions are. The trick (the very tricky trick) is to translate from numbers to poetry, from numbers into art.

Any artwork is framed by its physical self, whether that be the same as the last one made, or a new length or breadth. My next poem better not be one hundred thousand lines long, even were I so inclined. But timing is everything: these days I develop an idea of dimensions while I'm writing it, working out problems of line-length and stanza formation according to the poem's own devices rather than a pre-arranged rule. In my craft the portmanteau frame must be an elastic one. I would make it of clouds and feathers and, for every poem I put inside, I would take two poems back out.

He originally titled it 'Little White Girl'. First exhibited at the Royal Academy in 1864, Whistler's portrait of his lover, Joanna Hiffernan, inspired a poem by Swinburne, entitled 'Before the Mirror'. Presumably Whistler liked the poem as he had it printed on gold leaf and pasted onto each side of the frame. This and the other paintings for which she sat are pretty much the most complete record that now exists of Jo Hiffernan, apart from the biographical fact of her having existed and having been involved with Whistler. She may or may not have had a son by him, named Harry (mentioned in letters, but not recorded officially). She may or may not have left Ireland during the Famine, with a sister who later worked for her as assistant, and a father who drank too much. Whistler lived with her from 1860 to 1866 and painted her wearing a wedding band in 'Little White Girl', though they were not registered as man and wife. She is described as having worked as a kind of manager for him, organizing his accounts, scheduling his public appearances, managing the paperwork of sales. When Whistler went to Valparaiso for seven months in 1866 (possibly to escape a round-up of Fenian sympathisers — he was a known friend of John O'Leary) he gave Power of Attorney to Jo. Little more is known about her though it has been speculated that she modelled for Gustave Courbet (with whom she likely had an affair) and is the subject of his famous 'l'Origine du Monde'. Certainly he painted her in 1865 as 'La Belle Irlandaise'. That and a reference to her (if it was she) selling antiques in later life in Aix-en-Provence. Curious to think that though her life is framed in near obscurity and biographical fug we have intimate knowledge of her appearance including, possibly, her vagina.

Clearly Whistler thought better of the original frame for 'Little White Girl' (which sounds like a bit of a dog's dinner, truth be told), and had it removed in the early 1890s as part of what has been described as his 'great re-framing campaign'. In 1873 he wrote to his friend, George Lucas, 'You will notice that my frames I have designed as carefully as my pictures, and thus they form as important a part as any of the rest of the work, carrying on the particular harmony throughout.'[xvi]

He had meanwhile developed an aesthetic of framing, and he acquired the practice of stamping his frames with the same butterfly motif that he used as a signature on his paintings so that they were now marked out as artworks in their own right.

He designed and had manufactured what is now known and sold as a 'Whistler Frame', which typically featured a moulding decorated either in parallel reeding, or in undecorated, gilded flats. 'I am the inventor of all this kind of decoration in colour in the frames,' he wrote, again to Lucas, 'that I may not have a lot of clever little Frenchmen trespassing on my ground.'[xvii] It was Whistler who first exhibited in painted frames, with the gilded overlay rubbed and thinned to allow the colour underneath to emerge, and it was a short step from there to the Impressionists' taste for abandoning gilt altogether, to exhibit in plain, painted frames.

By the time 'Little White Girl' was re-framed it had also been re-titled: it was exhibited in 1892 as 'Symphony in White, No. 2', Jo Hiffernan translated to a notion of music, an abstract entity.

What happened the original frame is not recorded. What would you do with a frame that had gold-leaf poems on all four sides, that proclaimed the frame as belonging, body and soul, to one painting only?

Perhaps it got recycled, the gold leaf somehow purged of the poem, making it more generally useful, less specifically resonant. Perhaps it frames a different painting now, and hangs innocently and modestly on a wall that knows nothing of Jo Hiffernan or her lovers or her life. Or perhaps someone bought the frame as was, and had another painting commissioned to fit, that would illustrate Swinburne's poem. Or perhaps it lies in a warehouse somewhere, one of the empty frames unsold when the famous frame auctions by Christie's and Sotheby's and Bonhams shut up shop. Or perhaps it has gone to Paris, where such sales still exist, to gather dust that had once, perhaps, settled on the sheets of the bed painted in 'l'Origine du Monde', or indeed on the famous auburn hair of Jo Hiffernan as she arrived at 32, rue Hautefeuille, Courbet's studio, her body adequately covered, as yet only moderately disclosed.

In the *Guardian* of May 22nd, 2015, Jonathan Jones describes Courbet's 'l'Origine du Monde' as a 'clinically voyeuristic

1866 oil painting of a woman shown literally and solely as a sex object, with all distractions, such as her face, ruthlessly removed'. The cropping is indeed ruthless, shearing the figure of any context that might cushion or mediate. Instead of a context, of a depicted life, there is frame. The frame stands in for all that has been so emphatically excluded. It acts as a kind of obverse modesty screen: faceless and without clothes (other than a crumpled sheet) the figure portrayed is all genitals and no personality. It cuts her off so severely at the base of the neck that several critics believe that there is, literally, more to the painting that has been, at some point, removed. In 2013 Jean-Jacques Fernier of the Gustave Courbet Institute in Paris declared to the world that the missing section had turned up, and that a recently discovered painting of a woman's head (Jo Hiffernan's, he declared) was of a piece with this body, and had been clearly guillotined at some stage since 1866. *Paris Match* reported that the portrait was discovered by an anonymous collector among 'yard sale detritus' and then sold through a Parisian antique shop in 2010 for almost two thousand dollars. The report concluded that the painting is now estimated to be worth fifty-five million dollars. That's a whole other gilt trip.

The Impressionists cast off the cast, gilt frame. Gold tended to chafe against the soft oranges and yellows of their palette, and something that looked so overwrought undercut the aesthetic values of the movement. What they wanted were thin, pale frames, narrow strips of wood painted off-white or a neutral colour. What they wanted was an understated frame, nothing to distract from the drama of what it contained. By the time Seurat was painting his signature dots on the wood around the canvas as well as the canvas, and forbidding any additional frame, the frame was fair game: it could be treated as an extension of the painting instead of being a discrete device. It was subject to the requirements of the painting, and not to any set of aesthetic rules or practices that the frame might know more about than the painting: now the painting was in charge and the frame, designed by the artist, became a serviceable thing.

But what colours were the *right* ones: were there colours to best suit certain subject matter? Jules Champfleury, writing in 1882, thought so. He recommended green frames for landscapes, vermilion for dramatic scenes and pale grey for a woman.

Degas, invited to dinner once, noticed that the host, a collector, had changed the frame on one of his paintings from plain grey-green to fancy gold. Without a word Degas unhooked the painting, took the canvas from the frame and walked off with the painting, leaving his host (and patron) with only the frame to show for their friendship, and a cluttery gold frame at that.

The Die Brücke manifesto of 1906 claimed, 'we want freedom in our work and in our lives, independence from older, established forces'. Promoting spontaneity and freedom the group exalted colour and liberated line. Nothing was sacred, nothing taboo. At one point the group advocated smashing all picture frames, but Ernst Kirchner, the group's driving force and the manifesto's main author, continued to use in his own work a wide and simple flat frame in the major tones of the paintings it contained. Even ideology finds it hard to resist the claims and services of the frame: even when you most want to resist what it offers you can't help but articulate your objections in a firm and definite frame.

Some paintings seem to question the very premise of the frame, so that the frame is painted into the painting, its claimed space up for grabs. 'Portrait of a Man' (1520), of the Netherlandish School, shows a man leaning out over the lower part of the frame, his sleeve obscuring part of the wood. In Metsys's 'Portrait of a Woman' (1520) the woman is depicted between two sturdy marble pillars and, at the top of the painting, there is a gilt frame. Three sides are determinedly framed out but on the fourth, the bottom edge, the frame is tentative, the woman's pinkie seems to reach down into the painting's *beneath*, into the real world. Ingres painted flowers on frames. In his 'Portrait of Joseph Pembauer' (1890) Klimt uses the wooden frame like a scribblepad, with stars and a Greek pillar and two almost-doodled heads, even two fish drawn on. And on the canvas itself he writes words in gold, 'Anno Domini MDCCCLXXX'. All this around a painted head that is startlingly realistic, photographic, one might say. I'm not sure what is going on. It's as if Klimt doesn't trust his pinpoint accuracy, as though he feels the need to pit it against a different, more provisional style. Are the motifs purely decorative? Or are they commentative? Is the frame a complement or a contradiction? Later he painted many words around central images. 'Nuda Veritas' is topped by a substantial quote from Schiller. The effect is that of a poster, though the richness of the gold used heavily throughout says it can't be.

'A picture without a frame has the air about it of a naked, despoiled man. Its contents seem to spill out over the four sides of the canvas and dissolve into the atmosphere. By the same token the frame constantly demands a picture with which to fill its interior, and does so to such an extent that, in the absence of one, the frame will tend to convert whatever happens to be visible within it into a picture.'
— José Ortega y Gasset, 1893-1955[xviii]

In later life Charles Rouault is said to have amused himself by painting frames on his pictures. As these got excluded from the paintings' measurements his actions made for pretty skewed catalogue entries. Not the worst way to spend your old age though: if you find yourself unexcited by new work, make the old work look different, make it current, make it look new. Changing the way it presents itself changes how it is seen. It's the kind of intervention known to anyone who puts on a swanky dress or a well made suit for a wedding or a do. High heels alter the way you walk. A hairdo with a hundred hairpins affects how you hold your head.

But it has to stop somewhere, this way paint has of over-reaching its physical limits, of bleeding into its environment, frame and wall and all. Even if you're Josef Albers, paying consecutive homage to square around square around square, so the outer edge seems an almost random stop (if a square can ever be a full stop), the painting can't go on forever, it has to stop somewhere. Unless the artist decides to paint the walls of every room the painting will hang in, at some point the painting has to give up its wild ambitions and settle for being itself. Maybe the point of the frame is to stop the painting getting lost, to make it not want to get down off its wayward, wonky cross, make its way through the crowd of onlookers, and simply disappear.

'Framing causes sensations of three dimensions. It gives an illusion of depth, so I took a frame of plain wood and mounted my picture on it.'
— Piet Mondrian, 1943[xix]

Time was, if I happened to be rich, my clothes were designed for my body, were fitted and sewn to my measurements, and would need to be altered should I choose to pass them on to somebody else, to a different body. Likewise, the frame, which was originally designed and carved with a particular painting in mind. And then the frame, over time, came to refer to different things, such as the purse of the owner, the other frames around it, curatorial policy. The frame had a message all its own, in the way clothes do too, when they are not concentrating on just covering up and, sometimes, even then. Certain frames seem to wear themselves, the picture inside it being merely a prop that pretends to confer a function on it, to be its *raison d'être*. And so with clothes: the models become skinnier and skinnier, as if their frames were an unfortunate excuse for the clothes that have to be worn by some body, but the less of them the better. I could anticipate a fashion show where the clothes are worn by laser projections moving down the runway. At the bottom, *zap!*, the imaged bodies disappear and the clothes make their own way back to the dressing rooms, to hang themselves up neatly. But art doesn't seem to allow for quite the same imbalances. A craze for faux-rococo frames will be followed, inevitably, by another for plain white wood, thin, yes, but humble too, in a way a fashion model rarely is. It will understand its relation to its art as one of service, of functionality, and not personality. 'In this way, I brought it to a more real existence,' continued Mondrian, the real, for him, being the stand-out rather than the blend-in.

When Mondrian's aesthetic was adopted by Yves St Laurent into fashion some twenty years on (fashion working on a slower fuse than it likes to acknowledge, most of the time) his frame of plain wood became the body. His 'Mondrian Day Dress' of 1965 is now held in the Metropolitan Museum of Art, displayed, when it is, on the abstract human form of a mannequin, and further displayed in the two-dimensional words of the catalogue which declare the dress 'a feat of dressmaking, setting in each block of jersey . . . the semblance of the Mondrian order . . . to accommodate the body imperceptibly by hiding all the shaping in the grid of seams'.[xx] The body imperceptible, the unseen frame. Those of us who live inside bodies we judge imperfect will know the fascinating possibility of clothes that make us less visible. Black clothes, baggy clothes, fitted clothes, gaudy clothes, dowdy clothes, clothes abundantly accessorized or excessively tailored, clothes that are apologetic and doggedly downplayed. Understated or overreaching, uniform or cartoon — we hope (in all our innocence) that the clothes will distract from the view of the wearer, that the frame will be louder than what is framed, that our little disappearing act will disappear that part of us we'd rather be without. We hope that something integral to our very selves, something we don't take off at night, our smile, perhaps, or our eyes or hands, will make all necessary declaration, just as a good painting may defy a bad frame; the worst of us hidden in the grid of seams, the best of us, our boldest colours, simply made more real.

All frames, round, oval or four-sided, seem hell-bent on total enclosure. Why so absolute?

If a frame can be held in place with fewer than four sides, then why is the convention to have four? I suspect the choice is not functional, but philosophical. The way the frame surrounds the art, allowing for no leakage or egress, is a standpoint. It means the only way the art can have impact is through the space right in front of it. It's like cutting off all the stage lights except for one spot directly in front of the actor about to deliver a soliloquy.

If to the left of the frame is *before* (the past) and to the right is *after* (the future), what is it that top and bottom signify?

'No matter how unpeaceful the thing previous to art is — once it has been addressed and brought into a condition called art, it is, if not pacified, brought into equilibrium. For a moment, the parallelogram of forces is just held. The minute after art, everything breaks out again.'

— Seamus Heaney[xxi]

The frame is rarely the end of the story. As the painting rubs up against the frame the frame leans into the wall. And the wall is our wall. If you were minded to you could spray paint slogans on it, or crayon your name. It would be vandalism, certainly, but not, I think, criminal damage. I doubt you'd go to jail for writing on a wall that has no real intrinsic value other than its materials. In fact, you might even increase its value, especially if your name is Banksy. The wall is where the image can be contested, completed, rediscovered, reproduced. From somewhere behind it, from somewhere outside, the painted head separated from the woman's painted body might someday turn up (and did). The frame is only the halfway house, the indicator that there is, in the words of Coriolanus, 'a world elsewhere'.

Despite Whistler, despite Degas, frames, unlike the painting they shelter, are mostly anonymous. Where they are named it is as a type. Sometimes a type of frame is named for a framemaker, as in the Duveen or the Lely. Sometimes for an architect, as in the Kent or the Sansovino. Sometimes for the patron or collector, as in the Louis XIII or the Medici or the Herrera or the Sunderland (named for Robert Spencer, Second Earl of Sunderland and owner of Althorp, where Princess Diana was buried in 1997). And sometimes for an artist, as in the Rossetti, the Degas, the Whistler or the Gluck. Or the Watts, the Salvator Rosa, the Carlo Maratta, the Morland, or the Romney. Sometimes the frame an artist devised is the only thing that survives of him now and we know his name because the frame has currency; because it is used to house paintings he did not paint; because it's bought and sold as a thing in its own right; because the name signifies a look or motif and is not asked to recall a life; because the frame is sturdier than all his deeds and passions and zeal; because it's made of more durable stuff. Because we've found a use for it.

'The frame is always the sign of a lack.'
— Jean-Claude Lebensztejn[xxii]

When I moved to my new flat I put away all the framed photographs that used to hang on the walls of my last home. I keep boxes of them in a cupboard, frame after frame, row after row, like so many displays of butterflies in a natural history museum. I was the photographer, so very few of those family photos have me in them and yet they are the record of my life. I curated it. And I dismantled it to move here, to learn to live alone. No wonder I can't bear to look them in the eye.

Skylights in my flat frame the sky. The first thing I see upon waking is a square of sky. I think this is a good thing, the broad expanse presented in a manageable frame, already rendered and curated, pre-selected for me. It makes it easier to get up, this double-glazed sky; even the day seems possible: a thing of four corners and a view made available to me.

A frame concentrates the eye: it homes in and accentuates,

recognizes that being only human we are overwhelmed by too much detail, and all too inclined to surrender when too much is asked of us. I cannot begin to contemplate the totality of human suffering, but I can understand one take, one experience, when it is singled out for me in particular detail, as in the photographs of Sebastiao Salgado, or Dorothea Lange. The singling out asks a detail to represent what is bigger than itself, an essential symbolism. It's a trick of perspective, as in a Japanese garden where a boulder stands in for a mountain, a maple for thousands of trees. The frame tinkers with perspective: accentuate a detail by framing it and the rest of the story, no matter how clamorous or colourful, blends into the background. Our attention is a framing device and what we choose to notice can seem infinitely more significant than the full course of what we don't. But if what I place inside the frame of this writing becomes instantly emphasized, even exaggerated, then so be it. Perspective is tricky to get right, especially when your eye is pressed up to the life that, being looked at from any angle at all, seems instantly skewed. I think of the last stanza of Elizabeth Bishop's 'The Shampoo', what it does to perspective, how it brings what is very far removed so very close to home:

> The shooting stars in your black hair
> in bright formation
> are flocking where,
> so straight, so soon?
> — Come, let me wash it in this big tin basin,
> battered and shiny like the moon.

This confusion of distance and size can be one of the most intriguing aspects of naïve art. Though scarcely a naïve painter, Bishop's watercolour, 'Red Stove and Flowers', has a jug of flowers as big as the stove with its saucepans of stewing food and prominent stovepipe.[xxiii] And why not? Squint, and the proper order of things destabilizes anyhow. Bishop's paintings are full of frames, mirrors and pictures in literal (painted) frames, as well as fireplaces, windows, table tops, doors and books that seem to organize the rooms around them along parallel lines, the better to manage our attention and to direct the eye. Her paintings do as her poems bid, moving from detail to bigger picture with relentless dash. No one plays perspective better than she does. In 'Questions of Travel' she asks, 'And have we room / for one more folded sunset, still quite warm?', so the movement is in and down, towards particularity, quite different from that of 'One Art' where the sequence of lost things is ratcheted up (and out) — from keys to a watch to a continent to a lost love — with the breathtaking skill of a trapeze artist getting from the ground beneath all our feet to dangerous and dizzy high ground. I've always been struck by how she chooses to locate such personal material within the strict formal frame of the villanelle, just as in 'Sestina' the child draws a 'rigid house', and only then 'puts in a man with buttons like tears'. First comes a rigid form, then comes a kind of truth.

The body peddles an ultimate truth. It is some kind of frame for personality but it is a frail frame, subject to decay and contradiction. It knows its offer of protection is necessarily temporary. The wooden frame, on the other hand, offers order and permanence. It is crafty: it knows about commerce and commodities, mercantile values. It has no interest in being ephemeral; it has business to conduct.

Twice I have been pregnant, and twice I have given birth. My son and my daughter began as cells in the frame of the body I use now to write these words to include them again, my children, in the frame of my account.

My body is a practical support. I am fifty-one. It is not a beautiful thing, unless function trumps aesthetics, but it works, holds me together, keeps me upright and safe (for now) within my small place in the world. My body is a contemporary frame, of narrow but deep value, to myself at any rate. I value it, but I honour it according to its practical usage rather than for its capacity to dream. There is a little too much of it and, being fifty-one years hauling itself in and out of my days, it no longer allows itself (much) flattery or lies. And yet I like it, I am grateful to it. So far it has never refused me, it has held faith with me. I am on intimate terms with it. I live there. I inhabit it, probably, in much the same way as a painting inhabits its frame, but my body is a frame that doesn't know it's a frame. It just *is*. I am about different work, to which my body is indifferent. Something there is in me that tiptoes past its vigilance, that gets me by.

Every girl crosses a threshold into puberty and out the other side in her middle age. What's between is framed in a grid of months, each one roughly equivalent, twenty-eight days, more or less. You get to measure time by each square of the grid. Most of us keep some kind of record, a periodic table of one colour, red; each month carefully calibrated, except that the overall frame, the beginning and end, are harder to pin down. You don't know it's starting until it does, and equally the last, which you won't know is the last until there is no other. Eleven years or so before the first, who knows how many years after the last? These days, with the average female life expectancy running at eighty in Europe, most of us women can expect up to thirty years of no periods after the menopause. Of course we will expect them privately, the menopause being one of the very few subjects still considered faintly indecorous, not to be mentioned in public or, God help us, aired before men. This confuses me. It's one hell of a tricky threshold to be crossing in the dark.

Boxed up as a medical 'problem', a conversation for the consulting (as opposed to the living) room, the menopause (or the perimenopause — as it's officially known — the hard time before periods stop altogether and everything levels out) feels very often like a solitary confinement. And it feels like a punishment levied for all those years of wielding the power of fertility and childbearing. Like most punishments, one is often ashamed of it, however daft that is. I wouldn't be ashamed of a toothache or a broken finger or any, really, of the many ways my body might fail or bother me. But this feels personal, as though my body is not only failing me, but has actively turned on me.

The menopause puts me in mind of the *gae bolga* in the Ulster Cycle of myths, Cúchulainn's special weapon that would enter a man with a single wound and then expand into seven prongs with seven barbs on each so, when pulled out, it would scrape his guts along with it. Melodramatic, maybe, but I wonder if many women my age would consider the comparison false? The menopause feels as though the frame of my body is allowed to stand while all inside is pulled fiercely out of me. And not just blood, my whole sense of myself, my being me, and the way I have learned, these past forty years, to mark and occupy time.

I am minded too of those art thefts I have described elsewhere, the cutting out of a painting to spirit it away. Except that what's discarded in my case may prove, after all, the valuable bit, and what remains to me is to make do with only an awkwardly empty frame for the trouble of the heist.

Curious frame, this body of mine, that regularly breaks itself down. It is a frame made of blood and water and other malleable stuff. Even the bones are brittle at my age, I'm told (for fear I'd start to take for granted any solidity). Most frames stay put, but not my body that for forty years has reconvened once a month, and now decides to unstring me, as if to see what I'm made of. As if it wouldn't know.

In *A Voice from the Chorus* Andrey Sinyavsky (writing as Abram Tertz) invokes Cúchulainn's battle with Ferdia. He's plenty taken by the *gae bolga* ('the spear . . . went into three parts and pierced the clothes and stuck in the body, filling with its barbs every muscle and every joint of Fer Diad's body'[xxiv]), but what really seems to grab him is Cúchulainn's warp-spasm, the 'miraculous distortion of the hero in his frenzy': 'All his bones would be displaced and muscles would swell and become as big as a warrior's fist . . . His heart-beats were like a lion's roar . . . '[xxv] Distortion, transfiguration, unforeseeable and terrifying reinvention — it's not difficult to see why these would appeal to a man writing from a forced-labour camp (or 'corrective labour colony', to use the official designation) at Dubrovlag in Russia. Sinyavsky had been arrested by the KGB in September 1965, tried for Anti-Soviet activities (evidence of which was 'found' in his fiction) and subsequently sentenced to seven years, where he kept a diary of sorts — ruminations and observations mostly communicated in the twice-monthly letters he was allowed to his wife, Maria. How odd that Cúchulainn should find himself so very far from home, and yet not so very odd after all. Frames can be swopped out and changed about: context need not be everything. The myth abides because it is capable of being transferred from a field outside Ardee, County Louth, to a labour camp in post-Stalinist Russia, and for something of its essential truth to persist and to apply. In the myth Cúchulainn is powerfully released from the limited frame of his body. In *A Voice from the Chorus* Sinyavsky releases himself from the frame of his sentence, to a kind of imaginative transcendence: 'When all is said and done,' he writes, 'a camp gives the feeling of maximum freedom.'[xxvi] I'm not sure I could go quite so far, but then again I don't have to. I do know, however, there are times when compromise with one's body feels like a defeat. Poor and silly thing that it is ('soft and weak and smooth', as Shakespeare had it in *The Taming of the Shrew*), it oughtn't to be allowed to mark the limits of our selves. And it doesn't. But it does. But it doesn't. And it does.

The John Rylands Museum in Manchester has exhibited the shrivelled eyeball of John Dalton who discovered colour blindness (the French call it *Daltonisme*). The museum presents it in a Petri dish, framed in a glass case, as if the eyeball needs a clear view of everything that's around it, of its place in the scheme of things. It's odd to see an eye that is incapable of seeing yours. I looked right into it. Don't ask me what colour the iris is. I saw only the idea of the thing, the unlikely fact of its existence in a Petri dish, in a frame. I thought of Rembrandt's self-portraits, of those eyes of paint and canvas that seem able to look right into your own. Then I thought of the unpainted eye that shuts down when its supporting frame, its body, works no more.

See any open-plan office from a bird's-eye view, wouldn't it look like pictures hanging on a Victorian gallery wall? Every single person inside a frame; all the frames pressed cheek to jowl, and none of it very distinguishable, and none of it very distinct. But if everyone were to look up to meet the viewer's eye, wouldn't that change everything? The balance between frame and content would shift; the frame would become backdrop while the person inside would be the focus of attention, would be the only place you'd want to look.

Those artworks where painted eyes seem to meet the viewer's full on, how is it done? Take Rembrandt's late self-portraits, for instance. All that ferocious, unsettling honesty: it's all in the eyes and there's no hiding from it. If you're in the same room, from wherever you look, be sure they will meet your gaze. That gaze is not limited by the frame, it's not limited by anything very much, it takes no account of space or time; through centuries, through yards and metres, through eyewear and bustle and schedules and crowds, it seems to seek you out. And when it settles on you, it is to confront, upbraid, smite and unnerve. You are no longer a passive viewer; you are implicated by Rembrandt's vision of himself, which also seems like a judgement of you.

Despite the props, the hats and collars and cloaks and such, every one of Rembrandt's self-portraits seems to anatomize loss. Even the early ones. But the portraits from the last decade of his life are framed in tragedy and disappointment, and there was plenty of both. His heavy clothes and the shadows on his face are the seepage of a surrounding darkness in which he seems complicit. And the stare offers little relief. Meet those eyes, you get an inkling of the ways a life can fail.

An *inkling*. The word seems playful, as perhaps it ought to be. 'Accomplished fingers begin to play,' writes Yeats in 'Lapis

Lazuli' and, though he means they play the mournful music asked of them, we know he means play in the other sense too, since two lines later he is telling us, 'Their ancient, glittering eyes, are gay.' But Yeats's tragedy seems an abstract and not a personal one, and there is very little gaiety in those Rembrandt self-portraits. Framing misery in jollity is a challenging trick: like the blackness of the portraits it always seems to seep into light. Perhaps a strong depiction of loss can be made lighter by a gold frame, but it seems more plausible to allow darkness to stand its ground, even to the extent of the frame.

Though scarcely a confessional poet I write about my life. Impossible not to, really, since it's what puzzles me most. The lyric voice permits me to acknowledge that, when I write about frames, I may also be writing about my life and, conversely, though I write about what looks like my life I might as well write about any object that is both discrete and amenable, cordial and solitary. Much as any person is. Much as a frame tends to be.

Of the letters of the alphabet, only one works as a perfect frame. It is the O of the gold frame of Michelangelo's 'Doni Tondo', of the mouth in Beckett's *Not I*, the o of omphalos and origin, of globe and moon, of look and book, of for and good. Of open and store. Of close and lose. Of hole and whole. Of do and don't. Of hold and go. Of no and not. Of alone and know and so and old and, yes, love.

'Doni Tondo' ('The Holy Family') is Michelangelo's 1506 painting in the round. (In English, that *u* in 'round' seems like contraband: Italian with its rondo and tondo seems more on the money.) Though most round frames are made in four equal arcs that slot into each other I like to imagine that this frame is an unbroken circle, carved in the round, in a way that might be possible, albeit difficult. (Would you carve from a cross section? Would you try with water and steam, as with smoke and mirrors, to curve a flat plank round? How odd that wood seems to settle, as timber, for the flat. As a tree, wood has energy and range. It is full of surprises, you wouldn't know in what direction a branch will spring, or what notion a tree will take about height or girth. But as dead wood a tree turns literal: it commits itself to the most obvious ends. And the circular form, which confuses its end with its beginning, is an imaginative, even a metaphoric form.)

A round frame works as a gold ring does. And this round frame is a charmed circle, a protected place.

Within, an ordinary family: father, mother, infant son, arranged so their clothes and forms lean into each other, and so that the same colour is used for skin tones, like the same bass notes played under a wayward air, to establish a theme. They sit close in as if to shelter each other, this simple family that is anything but, that will be riven, in time, by fate and significance, but that here, in this early incarnation, is seen as an integrated whole.

'A sword shall pierce your heart,' the angel told Mary, and so it came to pass. The same sword might pierce the canvas to cut into three kinds of separate and absolute loneliness the three figures pictured here. Any canvas is vulnerable: it is only, despite the wild notions of paint, so much length and width of stuff. And any narrative can be unpicked, rewound to the point before it kicked in, returned to a state of full potential not yet compromised by what has to happen, by what will make this ordinary family the most wounded and compelling of all. This family, we know, will be all event: we learn its story the way we learn any story, scene by scene by scene. But in this painting a scene without narrative significance has been chosen: nothing happens (especially if you can ignore the hyperbolic naked figures littering the background). The family has been snatched from a story as portentous in terms of religion as it is fearsome in human terms: the story has been wound back and the family painted into a frame that is totally exclusive, admitting not a hint of threat to this ideal scene.

The round frame is a safe place inside which nothing terrible, it seems, will occur. It is a magic place: on the wall the round painting stands out marvellously, like poetry, defined by its physical self amongst the prose paragraphs of the more conventional frames to either side. Perhaps that is why the round frame is rare: you'd need a subject equal to the grand statement of the frame.

In many ways a circle (with its symbolism and metaphoric muscle) seems to command more faith than other forms, with their tiny chinks of doubt and weakness and reality. The circular frame is entirely committed to the painting it encloses: it follows no line of the room it is in and is likely to owe nothing to the paintings on either side. It doesn't mediate between painting and surroundings, or between fact and context: it is an absolute statement of adherence to the values of the art. But even that is a philosophical description, not an artistic one. (Then again the shape of the painting is very suggestive too, in how it looks like a globe, a mouth, a source, a womb. And the circle holds this family together in a way that its story will not.) I think we can allow it that philosophy, humility not being the strong suit of the gilded frame. Stripped of the right to dictate terms to the art it is asked to serve, a little intellectual display might be forgiven.

It also looks good. The complexity of enforcing curves on a substantial depth of wood, as well as its sculpted intricacy and its depth of ornament all mean that this is a seriously impressive frame. What strikes me most is the parity between painting and frame, how entirely complementary they are. It's as if there's no competition, no chafe between art and craft, or the art and its presentation. Call it holistic: art and frame together curve into the slip of that word (and other words that strike off it, namely *holy* and *whole*).

The two concentric circles of this artwork are like an emphatic full stop on the Uffizi Gallery wall. But with the nearby paintings more conventionally framed the wall could also be the dot and dashes of a message in Morse code. And the *tondo* looks, from the distance, like a breach in the wall, a round window, a porthole. If only you could find the right place to stand you could look through it, eye to eye, clear through to the sixteenth century, and you would know the place.

Insofar as a square can be a turning point Kasimir Malevich's 'Black Square' was. Its one-hundred-and-six centimetres squared includes the white border which was a new kind of frame in 1915 when the painting was hung in the '0.10 Exhibition' in Petrograd. It's a painted border around a square of black paint, same medium, same plane, same timeline, to the extent that Malevich thought of it as absent, 'a totally bare icon with no frame'. It's the logical progression of Seurat painting dots on the wooden frame, this making a frame out of paint. Not a frame in the sense of something added to a painting for presentation purposes, yet it looks very like a frame, especially when the painting is hung out of immediate eye-line, across the corner-join of two walls, high up under the ceiling, as an icon would have been in a Russian home. 'Black Square' connects two walls through an additional plane. It overrules the corner and it banishes the frame, and yet it works as a corner does and looks as if it has a frame. Black framed in white; black so the shape matters; black with something to say for itself. Call it abstract art, call it concrete poetry; call it iconic, either way.

Degas and Bonnard favoured a box frame — a flat border maintaining the surface of the board that backed the canvas, with the edge turned up at right angles. Very simple. Very clear. It's not a huge step from there to Joseph Cornell who took the box frame to a logical conclusion and made a box of it. The box became a feature of the art: the wooden frame he favours is highly self-conscious, declarative, and imposing — with the objects inside his boxed spaces pressing up against boundaries, or even pinned to their walls, they are fixed within its limits. In Cornell the box imprisons while it exhibits; closes down while it shows off.

Joseph Cornell put just about all kinds of everything there is inside a frame. Robert Motherwell saw a connection between the boxed objects and Cornell's obsessions which he listed thus: 'Birds and cages, empty cages, mirrors, ballerinas and theater folk (living and dead), foreign cities, Americana, Tom

Thumb, Greta Garbo, Mallarmé, Charlie Chaplin, neglected children, charts of the stars, wineglasses, pipes, corks, thimbles, indigo blue and milky white, silver tinsel, rubbed wood, wooden drawers filled with treasures, knobs, cheese boxes (as a joke), wooden balls, hoops, rings, corridors, prison bars, infinite alleys . . . '[xxvii]

What Cornell puts inside his frames seems to excite more interpretation than the frames themselves but, the way I see it, the point of his art is the frames. Without them there's just a random collection of objects; you'd see as much on the Show and Tell table of any primary school classroom. Everybody has a drawer of bric-à-brac that would give the treasures of a Cornell box a run for their purchase price. The found objects themselves are pretty much worthless but, when he puts them in a frame, Cornell confers a kind of associative worth on them into which we read all sorts. Inside his frames we see a magic space in which things become suddenly transformed into significance. Abstract ideas are made physically real: we work from the large abstraction down to the single detail, and back again. It's the motion of symbolism and, if the twentieth century taught us anything, it's how to negotiate between the concept and its manifestation, made horribly or wonderfully real. We like symbols; we think we know what needs to be done with them, how to shake them about like snow globes, to make them come alive.

Responding to Cornell is like doing sums: the clock spring equals the passage of time. The doll equals childhood, of course. The small glass jar of coloured sand equals a phial of gold dust. The answers are fairly obvious, and fairly satisfying when they come out right. And how do we know they're right? Because once we've discovered the key all the objects inside the frame can be unlocked with it. Childhood, we say. Loneliness. Time. Travel. Death. Loss. Destiny. It is the frame that makes the connections for us, that imposes whatever narrative there is, even if it's just symbolic narrative (which maybe is what all the best narratives are). The frames say, here are just these objects and no others, see if you can read them properly, make good sense of them. The frame or box is the story; the way I see it the objects inside are like illustrations of characters in a novel, but the frames are the words. To them falls the task of providing the rationale (call it 'the moral', if you will) on which the artwork hangs. Theirs is the real responsibility to make an environment in which magic can happen, and surreal connections seem terribly obvious, and association be a sensible way of making sense of any given situation. Like the shaman who draws a ring with a stick (within the border, a vision is possible; outwith, it is not) the frame marks off sacred ground. A dream-state. An altered consciousness. An altar, so that everything that comes in contact with it is sanctified and set apart and conferred with significance. Tear down the altar, scrub out the magic ring with your foot, take apart the picture frame, the space it had protected becomes ordinary. And something that had magic in it becomes something that had magic in it, and will not again.

Never much of a collector the closest I've come is a modest and entirely valueless assortment of wooden boxes. Some I use for storage, others are just pretty boxes, bought for their wood or their patina or some small eccentricity they have. I'm not especially a poet of death but my box collection can't help but nudge me in that direction. That box, the ultimate box, begins as the ultimate frame. Someday (assuming I don't die in a fire, bad crash or spontaneously combust) my body will be laid out in an open casket and anyone who wants to will be able to look at me. Like Dalton's eye, I won't be able to look back. They can make whatever they will of me (probably they'll say I look peaceful, or some other such nonsense) and then the lid will go on and they won't be able to see me any more. The frame will have become a box. Every frame is a potential box: when we look at a framed painting we stand in lieu of that final panel; we occupy, more or less, its space. When we look our bodies close the frame; when we move away we open it. If I were a painting I'd want no one to stand four-square in front of me, no one to block my light entirely or to threaten to close me off.

I wonder what a frame for my portrait would look like? It would have to be imaginary, as the portrait is.

At the Marina Abramovic show in Sydney (Project 30, Pier 2/3, June 24-July 5, 2015) the action is divided into acts that we, as visitors, as participants and collaborators, perform. These might be sifting black lentils from small mounds of rice, or lying on cots that remind me of field hospitals in WWI films. Or standing on platforms, still as we dare. Or staring into the eyes of a young woman I have just been paired off with. Or, in the final act, walking very, very slowly along a stretch of path, so our every step is broken down into a sequence of almost distinct and self-contained movements. I walked there for what felt like twenty minutes or so (you had to surrender your watches and phones when you entered the room) and gained maybe ten metres and a kind of out-of-body (and also intensely *in-body*) sense of feeling myself move in particular, miniscule and exaggerated ways. I felt as if my actions were broken down into a series of frames, rising, falling, lifting, putting down, balancing on one foot, then the other, then shifting my body effortfully into a space in front of me. Our silence accentuated the experience: there was no speech and we were given sound-muffling earphones on entrance. It wasn't like seeing myself in slow motion, it was *being* myself in slow motion, my relationship with time transformed and recharged. I wasn't sure what to make of it. I experienced my body differently as if, through acts of focus and deliberation, I might be a different me, perhaps a more careful and alert me. Leaving the warehouse where the show was housed, it was tricky to fall back into line with myself, to walk at a normal pace or to think back into the functioning tumble-dryer that is how I think, most of the time. It was disconcerting: I had visited a gallery space and I had been asked to look at myself in a series of frames that were not mirrors and were not glass, but were constructed from bits and pieces of my bodily functions that seemed more redolent and more significant than I. I use my body as a machine for living. This exhibition seemed to ask me not to, or at least not to do so carelessly, but to pay attention to the machine, to pour my life, action by action, grain by grain, back into the frame of my body, that I might live and have my being in an essential self.

Imagine constructing self-portraits for hundreds, maybe thousands of people. In the age of the selfie, imagine constructing one but once.

Hannah Gluckstein, known by her choosing as Gluck ('no prefix, suffix, or quotes') was heir to the Lyons tea-room fortune. Not being all that interested in catering (though sponsored by a generous trust fund from her father) she trained as a painter at St John's Wood Art School and cultivated a pipe-smoking, cropped hair androgyny that was not uncontroversial in its day. Her paintings — landscapes (usually featuring water channels of some sort), still lifes of flowers with an overtly sensual tone (she wrote of 'loving them and stroking them with my most chosen brushes') and portraits of establishment men and society women — brought her approval and success. Her double portrait of herself with her lover, Nesta Obermar, 'Medallion' (1937), celebrates what Gluck called their marriage on June 23rd, 1936, when the intensity and fervour of a performance of Mozart's *Don Giovanni* at Glyndebourne had, she believed, fused them into a single ('YouWe') entity.

In 1932 she designed and patented a signature frame, three white wooden bands stepped back from the picture, like very shallow steps out of a very shallow pool. She wrote: 'the usual essence of all frames was reversed and, instead of the outer edge dominating, it was made to die away into the wall and cease to be a separate feature'.[xxviii] 'The essential feature of the Gluck frame', according to a note in the catalogue of her 1937 Fine Art Society exhibition, 'is that it becomes part of any wall whatever its character, colour or period . . . It can be painted the same colour as the wall, or covered with the same wall-paper, or made in any wall material.'[xxix]

The frame was a great success, with articles in the *Sunday*

*Times,* the *Times* and *Tatler* commenting on its design and elegance. At the *British Art in Industry Exhibition* in 1935 the organizer, John de la Valette, used the frame without permission, claiming it 'the best frame he had ever seen'. Gluck considered the option of outrage but, upon seeing the exhibition in Burlington House, opted for flattery instead, and allowed the frames to remain.[xxx]

Like much else from the time — the mink stoles, the plus fours, the upper-class accent that could cut diamonds — the frame has not worn particularly well and is highly unlikely to be used in contemporary exhibitions. For a frame designed to blend in with the wall it draws quite a lot of attention to itself, with its three tiered flats. You could call it fussy and I imagine few paintings, aside from Gluck's own austere and accentuated work, could withstand its heavy-handedness. Its physical reality seems to be at odds with its design principle. You could call it a theoretical frame, this frame with a definition drawn more from ideas than from practice. And though I'm taken by the notion of a theoretical frame I can't quite imagine being able to balance its wilfulness against the competing claims of any painting it might contain. Too heavy, too threefold, too pronounced, it strikes me as having too much of a point to prove, and the point is uncharmingly instructional. The way the frame protrudes from the wall reminds me of a finger wagging, bossily, in my face.

In 1944 Gluck moved in with Edith Shackleton Heald, former journalist, parliamentary reporter and (last) lover of W B Yeats. In June 1947 the two women visited Yeats's grave, only to discover that the poet had been disinterred the previous year and his bones mixed with others in the ossuary. Gluck's biographer, Dina Souhami, recounts how Heald crouched on the floor of their hotel in Monte Carlo, sobbing and saying of her previous lover, 'I would know his bones anywhere.'[xxxi]

'"O cruel Death, give three things back," / *Sang a bone upon the shore*' ('Words for Music Perhaps', Part XV: 'Three Things'). But the bone wave-whitens and dries in the wind, nothing is returned to it, not the child, not the man, not the morning it invokes. Bones seem almost ghoulishly animate in Yeats's poems: they can be made to sing, to dream, to think. In 'The Collar-Bone of a Hare' the bones are a kind of medium, a way of throwing a voice of criticism. In the second stanza the narrator imagines:

> I would find by the edge of that water
> The collar-bone of a hare
> Worn thin by the lapping of a water,
> And pierce it through with a gimlet, and stare
> At the old bitter world where they marry in churches,
> And laugh over the untroubled water
> At all who marry in churches,
> Through the white thin bone of a hare.

These are bones to rattle death, not to commit to nothingness as Dylan Thomas has his bones do in 'And Death Shall Have No Dominion' when he projects to a time 'When their bones are picked clean and the clean bones gone'. Yeats's bones seem awfully interested in and committed to life. It seems apt, then, that his actual bones should be so rattled and bickered over. On July 18th, 2015, his bones made front page news in *The Irish Times*. An article titled 'Yeats: Papers confirm bones sent to Sligo were not poet's' drew on recently published French papers suggesting that the repatriated body was assembled out of the ossuary by local pathologist, Dr Rebouillat, at the suggestion of Bernard Cailloux, the French diplomat charged with locating Yeats's body in Roquebrune cemetery. It is as if Yeats's bones are still being made to perform, to act out a narrative of which they are entirely innocent. It is as if they have swopped the frame of the leaden coffin (the cost of which was repaid by the Irish Government to the French in 1948) for a narrative frame, a story in which they are made to sing like the bone of 'Three Things', to ask for something back, a story that is vexed and farcical, through which we may hear ourselves laugh a hollow kind of laugh.

The skeleton of the 'Irish Giant', Charles Byrne (or O'Brien, depending on who you believe) is exhibited in an eight-foot-high glass case at the Royal College of Surgeons in London in close proximity to that of Joseph Merrick, the 'Elephant Man'. These are idiosyncratic bones: the whole point of these skeletons is that they still attach to the story of two lives. Most bones do not: they look, more or less, alike and are, as the Yeats story proves, more or less interchangeable. (What does it signify, in the end, if a skeleton is made up of an assemblage of bones taken from various bodies? The act, in its way, is true to life, most of us living not one life in a dead-straight line, but several that loop into each other and duck and dive and overlap.) Look at any skeleton and you see a structural support that supports nothing, not even itself. When I see art frames without art inside they look to me like skeletons shorn of their living impulse, bones from which the marrow has dried. Yeats's 'A Prayer for Old Age' notes, 'He that sings a lasting song / Thinks in a marrow-bone'. Against this *The Dreaming of the Bones* notes that 'Dry bones that dream are bitter.' Dry bones. Empty frames. Nothing to say for themselves, nothing to sing, and only bitter dreams.

'Vacillation' shows W B Yeats in a moment of unusually low-register melancholy brought on by the middle age pinpointed in the lines, 'Between extremities / Man runs his course'. The first (five-line) sentence of Part IV deploys possibly the plainest diction and simplest description of any Yeats poem.

> My fiftieth year had come and gone,
> I sat, a solitary man,
> In a crowded London shop,
> An open book and empty cup
> On the marble table-top.

Of course it doesn't last. You might as well tell an Olympic high diver to stick to the paddling pool. By the end of the second five-line sentence the cup is overflowing and a single moment of cauterizing loneliness has been converted to twenty minutes of rhymed bliss.

> While on the shop and streets I gazed
> My body of a sudden blazed;
> And twenty minutes more or less
> It seemed, so great my happiness,
> That I was blessèd and could bless.

Middle-aged he might have been but Yeats wasn't one for doing things by halves. It was, in fact, all ahead of him, his best work, his sturdy marriage, fatherhood, a Nobel Prize in Literature, a term as Senator, a spate of valedictory and intensely pursued love affairs. If life can be said to turn on a sixpence it can turn on the marvellous full stop at the very middle of this ten-line section. It separates two sentences, two episodes, two moods, a dogged realism, a transcendent blaze. The full stop turns and a life does too: it is one of the most helpful punctuation marks I know and although, in Part V of the poem, he is weighed down by what he didn't do or say, and Part VI ends rather more sombrely, I don't mind about that.

> What's the meaning of all song?
> "Let all things pass away."

He could go his whole life shutting the book on that marble table-top (though he does not) and it wouldn't undo the moment when life seemed more a matter of openings than closings. And twenty minutes, God knows, is a precious long time for a moment to last. I'd swop a lot of days and nights for twenty minutes of that full stop upon which whole years, even decades, even the rest of a life, might come, in time, to rest.

What does it signify that when I go to a café, to be in the same place as other visible, breathing folk, I sit up at the street window with my back to the room and everyone in it? The café is behind me and to the sides; I can barely take stock of it. Instead I look out to a busy street and some of the passersby on that street glancingly meet my eye. I doubt they pay me much attention. If they do they look my way for a split second before looking away. I might register as a patch of colour or a scant detail not vivid enough, never vivid enough, to interrupt their flow of chat or their footfall. They walk on into the rest of their lives. I wait, suspended, for the next onlooker. I may wait a while.

What if this sadness has been in me so long it has seeped into my bones? I may have become it, so much so that I may never put it behind me or step away from it. No matter what luck or blessing comes my way it will make precious little difference because the sadness is such that I live in its thrall. It is, suddenly and totally, who I am. Not at all like a blur of shadow thrown for a moment on the glass of a frame, a fleeting darkness that will shortly rub itself out or simply lift. Maybe my sadness has altered my chemistry, as light will do a watercolour, and has changed me, drained me, so I am a paler, less vivid version of myself. I might have protected myself against it once, as I have done with my two water-colour paintings, framed against ultraviolet light.

But what would protect against sadness? Surely not happiness, that most fragile and porous of feelings. Luck, perhaps. But luck can't be applied like a coat of varnish: if we could manage it it wouldn't be luck. Love, perhaps. But oughtn't even unloved people to be not sad sometimes? Perhaps mindfulness, attention given to the world? But the world is also furious, thwarting and disappointing: one would do well not to look to the world to avoid sadness. Hope? Maybe. But I'm not sure I can train myself to the practice of it. Beauty? But beauty carries in it a seed of sadness, the knowledge of its inevitable passing, the momentary stay against death. I don't know what the answer is. Perhaps it lies not in opposition. Perhaps the protection against sadness is a greater sadness, in much the same way as a frame will pick out from the painting within a line of colour to accentuate. I might, when I was younger, have framed myself in sadness as a way of keeping that strain of myself fixed in position, held in check. But I never thought to try that out. I thought I could live in my family, my one safe, unsad home.

Or maybe it isn't sadness at all but a loneliness that does more or less what a frame does, an effective sealant, a border patrol under strict orders to allow nothing in, nothing out. Within it is a yearning, raw and visceral; beyond it is indifference, or what looks very much that way. Beyond it too is life, other people's lives, bristling with happening and dazzled with pleasure and claim. Inside is less vivid or more arid day on day. Loneliness is a great stifler: it muffles and drains and fades and restrains. It is a room with manifold padding against which you could fling yourself a thousand times and again, and your body would leave no imprint nor your being there make any mark.

Where does the colour go that has faded? Is it claimed by light and recycled there, in slips of exuberance?

Privacy trumps loneliness, or thinks it ought to. While loneliness is sobbing its heart out in the loo, privacy is wearing a plum velvet gown in a splendidly empty salon. Privacy meets the knock on the door with a 'Not now, darling'; loneliness can't help shuffling over to listen for breathing on the other side. Privacy admires the gilding on the frame it commissioned around itself; loneliness wastes hours wondering how the frame might be dismantled, if one only had the tools. Privacy says, I am private. Loneliness tells itself lies. And some of those lies become fictions. And some of those lies become poems.

Maybe the most honest frame, being the most humble, is the frame that is cut out of the wall, so the painting sits flush with the plaster. I always think Monet's 'Les Nymphéas' are hung this way in Musée de l'Orangerie in Paris and am always surprised when they're not. This museum was built to house these paintings, so it would make a kind of sense if the walls were, in fact, constructed around the artworks, so to speak. But no, these two sets of waterlily paintings (the two most beautiful rooms in Europe?) are hung in thin gold frames that have been rounded to fit the curve of the oval walls. The frames are not imposing, but they are there. And I wish they weren't. I love these rooms so much that I want to believe they are, literally, one with the same world I live in. Not separate from it, by even so much as a thin gold frame, but inherent to it, on the level, of a piece with it. I want my eye to be able to slip between white wall and Monet's fierce colour without having to register even this interruption, this threshold. Perhaps this is idealism, this notion that one can slip breathlessly, effortlessly between the 'real' and painted worlds. Maybe this is what the frame does: it gets me from the world at my back, a city teeming with style and occurrence, some of it ugly or grubby, some of it glamorous or swizz, to the meditative and transcendent beauty of these canvases. Thank heaven for them, so. Step into the requested silence, step over the threshold. Leave your city at the lip of the frame; like a garment stepped out of lightly, the city falls away from you, and you have been released.

In Jasper Johns' 'Canvas' (1956) the frame, painted in the same way as the canvas, has been included *inside* the painting. The frame frames an inner core that then extends, regardless, on a slightly higher plane, beyond the four edges of the wooden frame. It is not separate, not a discrete commentative or illustrative device, but is implicated in the business of the painting itself. It has been brought in from the cold. And it has been neutralized and disempowered. If a painting frames its frame what is the frame for, what does it mean? This painting unsettles me. There is me and there is not me. If not me becomes suddenly (by a realignment of reality) me, then what am I?

'I holp to frame thee,' says Volumnia in Shakespeare's *Coriolanus* when she wants him to act contrary to his instinct and judgement.[xxxii] She uses the word in the way we describe the framing of an argument, how it is outlined and given shape. She is a mother who has framed her son, has influenced his personality, informed his values, helped to define how he must define himself. But Coriolanus acts against her wishes and lights out to seek his impossible world elsewhere. Coriolanus seeks to fashion his own frame, partly of her devising and partly of his own. Fair enough. I have been framed, I know it, by my mother's melancholy, but also by my father's lack of it. These two stand to my mind as oppositions, like two parallel struts of frames. I am both. I am positioned between them. I am held in place.

'I holp to frame thee.' Volumnia means more, I think, than the body of the son she has nursed, but the body is first and foremost. It is the primary frame. Here, though we also exist in the round (some more than others, believe me), we also occupy two planes, define ourselves by two sets of fundamental dimensions, height and width. But there is another distinction too, that the body as frame cleaves to. There is My Body inside the limits of which is everything I am. And there is Not My Body outside of which is everything I am not. But Not I doesn't keep to itself: it allows itself to be tasted, seen, touched, heard and smelled — it enters and becomes me. I give myself to the Not I with every glance and movement that I make. And the Not I, in turn, rubs itself, so provocatively, so tenderly, so ruthlessly against me all the time. In the Not I, I live and breathe and move and have my being. Like a fish in water the Not I is my element. The tension between them, this balancing act, is the nub of me.

Say this morning I have a toothache into which my entire body seems to want to climb. The opposite of an out-of-body experience, it would seem I am ninety-nine per cent toothache, only one per cent me. When I switch on a lamp or climb the stairs my arm hurts or my foot does, nothing wrong with either of them. But my tooth trumps my body right now and so, until the dentist opens, I am defined by pain.

Though having dimensions, a cost and a history that can be tallied in dates, the numbers that define a frame are superficial truth. Size is relative: largesse and largeness are full rhymes and even a picture frame exactly the same size as the picture might prove less substantial and less arresting, if the art is good.

But the metaphor backs me into a position I'm not sure I like. I've made art be the toothache and the frame be the body (worse again, *my* body) that the pain soaks through. I think I may have overstretched the analogy, but that's pain for you: nothing in proportion. Whole hours fed into its maw. Nothing as it should be. You don't know where you are.

Here are all my perfect selves, frame by frame by frame. Some look out at the world, of course, some cannot or don't want to, and some don't know where to look. I could make a show of myself, this version and that version adding up, between them, to some kind of storyboard. But I resist. I don't think I want a narrative, however partial or skewed. I am maybe younger now than I was ten years ago. Nothing moves in straight lines, at least not that I can follow. I know much less than I'm sure I knew, and I have put away more; I see in smaller glances and I want for so much less. There is no discernible progression; there is nothing it all adds up to that is worth the tallying. And yet. A reckoning always seems to want to try to impose itself.

I think I live inside myself, all my versions and moments fitted one inside the other like a sequence of frames fitted corner to corner, side by side, angle to angle, barely a hint of daylight between. It might look, I reckon, as though you could lift any single frame out, to create some breathing space, to make way for a little light. But you couldn't. The whole thing works as a unit: its physics and craft and composition depend entirely on everything cohering tightly in its ordained place: move any one element a fraction and the whole thing would collapse.

Picture it, maybe, as a cross section of a complex Matryoshka doll, but with each wooden skin fitted snug, watertight, between its encompassing layers. No. First, I must take out every doll, set them in a row. The largest is the most readily recognizable version of myself, what the world knows to be me. The smallest is a bauble, an indeterminate personage with abstract features in disarray. Which one is the real, the very nub of me? Perhaps it depends on my say-so, there being no one in the world to gainsay or correct me.

How will I tell real from more real? And does it matter in the least? I fashion myself in onion layers but the difference between them is a matter of light and slightly different form.

Are there really different mes (how odd, that plural!) or simply different versions of a single me?

(All these questions fit into each other: I imagine the curl of the question mark crammed with planed questions like kittens curled into each other, until there is no white page left, only a clamorous, unanswerable, interrogatory ruck.)

Here I am in all my guises, each one composed and selected, each one true to form. I can make it so every one seems real, I know how that is done. Each one credible and self-contained, painted so it looks like all the others, but with an incremental difference of scale, a slightly different notion of how to occupy its frame.

There's me in the classroom, in the kitchen, in the music hall, on a coast road bending down to the sea. Me in an apron, me in a smile, me in a vintage black dress. Me with a book. Me with a notebook. Me out walking the dog. Me in a photograph, me in a mirror, me in somebody's mind. Me in love in my young day. Me before ever I knew of love, and me, years on, giving it up and wanting, badly, not to. Me on a rock with a child's fringe and a cardigan with white hens on it. Me swaddled in voices in a house with leaky windows and milk jugs and daffodils. Me with two babies and a husband and a light blue sitting room with a cast-iron fireplace lined to either side with books. Me in a tall Edwardian, wondering how on earth I was going to keep it up. Me passing myself off. Me polishing my mother's brasses. Me putting in time.

But how may I decide the sequence, or know how to arrange myself? What comes first, the earliest? Should it be at the centre or the outer edge? Should the final frame be the latest frame, or the one with most knowledge of the world around, that knows best how to deal with it?

I find I cannot make these frames fit snugly, one in the next. When was I *most*? When I was loved most? When I was younger and had what strikes me now as fathomless desires? When I had two children in need of so much I had to grow into the giving? When I had words on the go, the way they had of accruing into themselves (which was more than me)? Or when I made my peace with all manner of loss, and let so much fall from me? It's possible (just) that I am more than I used to be, so why does it seem like less? Like the scarf that is knitted so very long it can never be worn, perhaps I have learned the art of being me in time to find there's no real use for it. Perhaps I outgrew myself with the world when my body ceased to be potential and had to settle for age.

Or maybe all my frames are interchangeable, growing or contracting to the size required at any given time?

Here is me writing this, being more than I've ever needed to be, making much of myself.

Slow nights, hear me shuffle these small bits of knowledge and ignorance, so they sound like so many sticks being moved, in darkness, around. Their noise is the air shifted by a key turning in a lock. Or the onion layer of air between photographs in a closed box. Or the dead air that falls in behind a question there is no answer for. Or the air after music has finished, perhaps, one box of sound clicking tightly shut while another opens, shyly, imperceptibly, around it.

The Lely Frame, aka the Panel Frame, was a late seventeenth-century frame of carved floral corners and contrasting plain panels with no ornamental motif centred on each side. These panels are like a little rest for the frame, a moment to put the feet up, to not have to shimmy and whirl. Four pauses. One way of stopping the frame upping its own ante and losing the run of itself. They look to me, for all the world, like little stanza breaks. Busy into the corner, busy away, then half-way up to the next tricky ninety-degree angle, take a moment for an intake of breath. A lot can happen in that breath: the story might think better of itself, something significant might happen offstage and, when the next stanza kicks in, the ground has shifted slightly and the poem has realigned. Stanza breaks smuggle the white space around the poem into the heart of it. They are subversive and a good poet uses them to move the poem on a secret fraction that can matter a great deal. The stanza break knows how to ride roughshod over time: whole centuries, whole minutes can dissolve in its white-out. Death can happen and nothing can happen, and not a word be said. The stanza break makes the poem on the page look like a diagram of a pulse: there is life and then recess, and then another flurry. It is like the way we live in phases, the way we expand and contract. A stanza break might be as good a place as any to lie low. Come back again when the words come through, when they have recovered themselves. There is a time for everything, says Ecclesiastes 3: a time to scatter stones and time to gather them . . . a time to embrace and a time to refrain from embracing . . . a time for keeping and a time for discarding . . . a time to be silent and a time to speak.

I once wrote a poem about, I suppose, the break-up of my marriage. It's called 'X' and is much preoccupied with the shape of the letter and with how I once found in its four equal lines an equivalent of the four parts that made up my family. Rearrange those lines, of course, and you have a frame. Like many others I think I saw my family, my marriage, as a safe place, framed off and protected from the usual bothers of life. But the frame dissolved. Wood into water; water into steam. Perhaps there is no such thing as a safe-place. And even the most secure of frames is easily replaced.

What is my frame, what frames me? Is it my skin, my clothes, my room, my house, my city, my country, my continent, theworldtheearththemilkywaytheuniverse? At what point does my frame become everybody's frame? Could I touch the dividing line? Could I live inside it?

Turner liked his paintings hung in groups, without intervals between the frames, so that the overall impression was one of overwhelming light. I can barely remember but I imagine that is what falling in love must feel like: gold to your gold, everything around more splendid for its bloom.

My mother once claimed that she could find me a better husband than I'd find myself. I was young then, maybe twenty or so, and I said (and I'm sure I was righteously firm), not me; I'd never get married, marriage was done for. Well, I did get married, a decade later, to a man I chose for myself, but it ended anyway, and the ending fairly much gouged out my life, as such endings tend to do. Now, years on, it's too late for husbands, too late for many things (even things I want) and yet, sometimes, I find I want to say to her, 'well, go on then'. The fact that she is more than twenty years dead doesn't seem to prevent me. But I think my mother must have given up on husbands, at least for me. She tells me, in my own voice, that such things don't matter so much in the end. So I write about picture frames and forget about husbands. And I come to see the extent of my life as a surface with many words written on it, a scroll the same colour as the table it rests on, with no edges visible, and I can't quite see to the end of it, and I can see nothing past.

The first house we bought didn't exist. We bought it off the plans. It was a house on paper, not all that different from any house I could write into the world. I could say it would have so many rooms and so many windows, and the garden would be, *hey presto*, just like this. And I could make it happen, because that's what writers do: they build fictional houses with fictional lives and they screw on door handles and put down a rug and leave an envelope on a desk to make it real.

We built a house. It had a red hall and a yellow kitchen, and every room was perfect because we wanted it to be. Our dream house. We didn't quite believe it (give two writers a choice of a house on paper and a house with drains and permission and a view, watch them tally the losses and gains when the dream turns real). And so we built the perfect version of our house between us that wasn't hidebound by engineering but was pure potential, barely two narrow, terraced storeys away from lives that would keep us safe.

Our parallel house. The other one, the bricks and mortar one, kept pace with us, more or less. We'd paid a deposit with some money my mother left me when she'd died two years before. It was, I suppose, an inherited house, passed down through generations, though it had yet to become real.

I was pregnant then with our daughter, our son was not yet one year. My first book of poems had been published when I'd been three months pregnant with him; my husband's the year before that. We lived in a coastal village and played with Tommy and looked forward to Eve and wrote poems every day and that's all there was to it really, and it was enough. Once a week we'd go to town to view progress on the house, a little pilgrimage on a bus that kept to the coast road and picked up women with chickens in boxes and men with flat caps and carrier bags and the same words every time. That bus journey was like carrying a lucky stone in your pocket to make the day turn good. We'd wheel the buggy from the bus stop down to the site, a gaggle of family, more anxious than was necessary, to stand at the barrier and wonder if it would be ready by the time Eve was born. We'd talk to the foreman, worry about dates and schedules, and then go home to our rented flat to build this new house between us, word by word, flourish by flourish, inch by verifiable inch.

We were No. 7 of fourteen houses and they were going up collectively, layer by identical layer. They seemed so small. With the foundations in and levelled off the house looked less convincing than the paper plans. (It's hard to imagine vertical space if you're not used to it.) Exterior walls, roof, windows, I forget the sequence now but I remember, when the frames for the stud walls went in, the house seemed finally possible because now it had a notion of rooms. Like Chekhov's gun, once rooms had been set out, I knew our lives would make use of them.

From then on it was a matter (for us) of finishing touches, where plugs and radiators would go, and the dresser and the fold-over table, what pictures on what walls.

We lived in that house for seven years, and it was a good house, our best. Maybe if we'd never left we'd somehow be there still.

Of those seven years' worth of milestones, first steps, first haircuts, first days at school, this is the one I choose for a frame of words in the here and now. One day in a being-built Windmill Court, with the A-frames of fourteen roofs and the frames for the stud walls finally up, the foreman let us walk around, to get our bearings, he said. I stood there, my daughter inside me, my husband with our son in his arms in his knobbly blue cardigan, and I put my hand to the wooden slats that said where rooms would be. It was early spring and the sky was glazed with celadon, an ancient Chinese sky removed improbably to Dundalk. Light blue sky and yellow wood: a family with history and a future made visible, frame by frame, as somewhere we would live our lives. And us, believing in it.

All my houses: every one a stage set, page and frame. *To house*: (verb) to keep safe, to store . . . My childhood home with its hatches and folding doors that rarely opened. Various flats with their single beds and then, at last, a double made of two singles pushed together. Flats with coin meters and linoleum. Houses with hot presses and saucepans that matched. Then houses with our names on bills, our pictures on the walls.

Houses we moved into and out of again. Houses that remember us, if they do, as a layer of paint under more recent layers, a set of curtains made for a window, a dent on a skirting board. Houses we have photos of, kids on steps with the new dog, birthday cakes with candles lit, Christmas trees and painted toenails. A play in the back yard.

More. Listen. Maybe much more. Perhaps we never left. A house plays chimes like champagne flutes, has hinges that whinge, doors that slam like arguments, dark corners that sulk and slump. The boards of every floor we crossed may hold our weight in their creak and bounce. Perhaps every one of these houses retains in its air (that is never quite fresh) particles of our breath.

Walls are stuffed with horsehair and floors sometimes have skulls underneath: why not bits of us also, bits of our history? Dust from our skin in carpet pile and an earring lost, oh, decades ago, lodged in the curl of a drain. A shadow where a sorrow imprinted itself, or a window sill that always seems sunny because of a kiss that happened there. Scales from a keyboard that the stairs learned by heart, up and down and up and down again. Mirrors that kept back something of us from the reflections they gave out. A corner of the window frame where sounds of lovemaking still stir themselves to high notes, windy days.

Perhaps nobody dies in houses, not really, not completely. Perhaps wood and glass and fabric and all retain an impression of every life lived in its rooms, however scant, just as every picture frame may wear a trace of all images housed by it. Sometimes this is physical — a frame will have staples and pins that have no business being there. Under them, maybe, a coloured canvas thread that bears no relation to any colour in the picture now in place. Or damage where one painting has been roughly removed and another slotted in place. An echo of paint.

Sometimes, yes, it's physical. And sometimes, no, it's not.

When I left the last house I lived in that might have been called a family home my daughter took a photograph with her polaroid camera. I am standing at the front door and the lilac tree (which the new owners cut down) is still in bloom. The film was old stock and the photo never really came out true. My figure is the clearest thing in it, you'd know it was me, squat and transitory, almost out the door, while the house — that tall, substantial, aged house — bleeds out at the corners into the polaroid's white frame. The last day. A few more hours and I'd be gone, moved on, new owners in place, all bustle and novelty, and maybe even a photo called for, all the family out on the front step. Someone says, Smile. And the house, that already has the measure of them as it did of us, that has processed so many firsts, the comings and goings, the ins and outs of more than one hundred years; this house that knows more than any of us and will see many more of us out, this house either presents itself full on to all this new-strung life, or it doesn't (as in my case) and instead, more backdrop than frame, it holds back, feint and indeterminate, as if to play a waiting game.

In his account of a dying way of life on a Hebridean croft, *Night Falls on Ardnamurchan*, Alasdair Maclean recounts a game described to him by a one-time seafaring neighbour. 'Jack All Alone' involved a crew member of a ship taking himself forward onto the bows of his ship, climbing out on to the bowsprit, and lying there on his back for as long as he could bear it. 'What the player waited for,' Maclean writes, 'was for the great rush of wind and water, the tearing sky overhead, to have their inevitable effect on him, to crush him into an unendurable awareness of his own smallness and loneliness.'[xxxiii] I hardly knew what a bowsprit was when I read this passage, I had to look it up. And when I did the full terror of the experience, of what the men were daring themselves to do, came home to me. The bowsprit is the pole that extends from the ship's prow, to which the stays of the fore-mast are fastened. Lie on your back on that in darkness, with ungovernable weather and fathomless dark letting loose all around you, and you will feel for sure alone. The winner of the game was he who could stay longest. Nobody, the neighbour said, tended to last very long.

I was tempted, when I read this, to name my new flat 'The Bowsprit'. At the top and edge of my building and with the sky its best company through its several skylights, it knows the weather, or it thinks it does. Here I live alone for what I have recently realized is the first time in my life. Times, truth to tell, loneliness seems like something about to crash down over me. I have allowed myself, on the odd occasion, to feel close to being overwhelmed. But it is a relatively simple thing for me to climb down from it too, to meet a friend for coffee, Skype my kids, to see a film or find my way out, link by link, along music's fine gold chains. This is how I surround myself with a frame I recognize: I simply put myself back in it, by an effort of will. God help me if that will should fail for I've seen beyond the edge of the frame, now and then, enough to make me turn on my heel, lower my gaze and strike out for whatever comfort I know will give me safe haven for as long as it takes to not feel so alone.

'Jack All Alone' moves the will in the opposite direction, towards a terrifying solitude, not away from it. The player of the game climbs out of the frame of the known in the most visceral way I can imagine. Beyond that frame is terror and danger both physical and psychological. We are not made to be so alone and so vulnerable: we're only small. We can only take so much out there, where the unknown threatens to topple our very sense of ourselves. I wouldn't last a minute playing 'Jack All Alone'. I wouldn't have to: one look at the spar hanging all on its own, I'd have bolted for below deck where I'd be putting on the kettle, reaching for a memory with no adventure in it, and no loneliness.

Holiday snaps. Cupboards full of them and thick albums, year on year. Sitting-room walls of them in frames, clustered souvenirs of what looks like happiness. The holiday itself gets framed in memory, so the sun shone, the humour was good, it was a happy time. We're great ones for doing that, for slapping an imagined frame around what we don't want to disappear. We do it to our youth. We do it to love. I do it all the time.

It's the strangest thing about living alone, I think, the way you have to purposefully seek out what might make you laugh. I've seen all kinds of frames, from the downright ugly to the guilelessly elegant, but I've never seen a funny frame. I may have lived a sheltered life.

Part summer house, part shack, with no central heating back then, and no fireplace, the chalet was for Easter and August and warm weekends between. Winter, it lay idle, the windows closed and the door locked fast, the grass growing whenever it had the energy, no car slowing to the hidden entrance, no child running to roll back the stone that blocked the lane we used for parking. And then, with longer days, there came us, pushing our voices out in front, carrying in bedding and swimming togs and saucepans and groceries and coats. The first job was to deal with mattresses left fallow for six months. That meant dragging them out onto the grass and applying liberal doses of DDT shook out, as I recall, from orange, tin cylinders, the chalky smell of it clashing with sea air and fine spun light. Fleas and God knows what dispatched, we'd drag the mattresses back inside, thereon to dream short summer nights of clear skies and suntans. We didn't know about the wildlife DDT had under its poisonous thumb, the eggshell thinning that drastically cut the numbers of falcons, condors and hawks; the ruinous effects on bats and fish, how so many species would revive only when DDT was banned in the early '70s. We thought what we did on a patch of grass with summer mattresses from a summer house was nobody's business but our own, and if anyone had told us we were organisms living amongst other organisms we'd have trimmed that conversation short for who, on an evening in Connemara with the car unpacked and the beds made up, would choose to spend time with a crank? But our actions were not discrete. Us shaking DDT over mattresses there was part of something with a fearsome geographic and environmental reach. Sometimes, I know now, with the benefit of age, the frames you put around actions are purely illusory. Choice knocks against consequence all the livelong day: there is no length or breadth of wood that can separate me from that. The mattresses went to landfill, I reckon, and we grew wiser, learned a thing or two. And those summers, every one of them, spent themselves as summers do, and some of us died and some of us stack up years like so many saucers. The light I live by is already seventeen years old before it hits my eye. The breath I breathe has already passed though countless living organisms. So with words. Though I live alone what I write here are words that have passed through thousands of lungs and thousands of mouths. And when I die the body I have the use of now will seep into soil and water that fetches up elsewhere.

There is, I think, ultimately, no line to mark the limit of I am. This is my life, unframed. This is my life, not as a single, coherent, discrete thing, but as a thousand, a million things, brushing up against each other as so much dust in summer air, as so many drops of rain.

It occurs to me, writing this, perched in a blue room over Galway Bay, that the perfect frame, the most faithful and painstaking frame, is in fact the sea.

I grew up in the middle of an island, about as far from the coast as it is possible to be. But still not very far. An hour-and-a-half got us here, saucepans rattling in the boot of the car, old songs rattling in the front. Days, then, of cold meats and rummy, three swims a day, books for the rain, Nivea for sunshine, and sudden turns off back roads to sit on a flat stone under a busy sky for the length of a thin cigar. All winter was waiting for the weekend when we could turn the stiff key in the lock again, turn out mattresses, unflutter the cards and drink stronger tea. And all summer dreaded the end of August, the pull of the door behind us for another dark six months.

The year folded neatly into two equal halves, an inland one, all long nights and school hours and *Blue Peter* on TV, and its opposite, when Friday night was a quick run west and there was extra light in the sky before us to see us on our way. When Friday night was an open door to a brighter, jazzier room.

That stopped when my father died, the month before I turned thirteen.

(There's a painting over the fireplace, an unframed oil: a beach scene to the front, mostly yellow and blue, and then, at the four sides of the canvas, an inch of unpainted white before the blue of the wall kicks in.)

It had been his place and coming here without him was no fun. It seems it wasn't the place that mattered, but him in it, making a holiday of three rooms.

It took having children ourselves to bring us back to it.

And here I am, in January, courtesy of central heating and a ferry that brought me across a sea that was nothing like the one I stare at, over my laptop, now. Today the sun is arthritic, making a creaky entrance an hour ago to the left of the bay. Since then it has whinged in downpours, flat in itself; no fizz, no yellow to this heavy day.

The sea looks grumpy this morning. It's never good news when the bay is the same colour as the road. High up as I am, the Clare side looks on a level with me, as though it would take a very little tip for the whole shebang to spill over on us and for the sea to close, as Ovid wrote of Icarus, over our clamorous mouths.

In summer men will fish for mackerel from the flat rocks at the end of the lane. There will be yachts and the boat to the islands and possibly, some evening, a liner will inch in its crystal frame towards Galway as though it had taken a wrong turn out on the Atlantic and now is brightly dithering about what happens next. But for now what light there is comes from the flashing buoys of a wave energy experiment. And cars sprung as if from a trap on the far side of the bend.

I keep a low lamp lit all day. And fire by night for the sound of it, its one-liners and rambling tales that all finish the same way. Between cars I hear waves down on the foreshore paying the same old compliments, nightly, to bored stones. Fifty-one years I've been listening to the drag and swagger of them. So much has changed, but never that. New houses built between here and the view, more traffic on the road. People I loved who died or dropped, like stones themselves, out of the bottom of my life. Gains too, of course. (Oh, when did I acquire all this equanimity?)

I try to bring my life here at least once a year. It comforts me to set it in a frame it knows full well. The blue room is propped like an eastern gemstone in a setting of grey and green. Some days it seems like the grey sky is hell-bent on climbing through the windowpanes to contradict the blue. But mostly it finds other distractions: this evening they are slate roof tiles and the house foundations over the road, remembering lunchtime's rain. The bay has levelled to a sheen — you could take it for glass laid edge to edge between the rocks of Galway and the hills of Clare. You could even take it for glass laid edge to edge over the past fifty-one years.

In the chalet there are framed photographs of my mother and father on a hill. It will have been the '60s and they'll have been in Connemara, on a drive one summer day. (The photos we choose to frame, mostly, are lit by a sun that's enjoying itself, a vigorous sun, a summer sun, sun on a drive to Connemara, full of the joys, sun on a spree, sun that is sun to the hilt.) My mother photographs my father, then they change around. My mother wears a headscarf and her yellow blouse. She has glamour about her, the way she did. My father has his arms crossed, the way he did. They smile for each other, and the hill seems to lean into that smile. The whole day does.

My sister framed these photos from copies but the colours didn't hold. My mother, my father, the hill, the sky — they seem to have forgotten themselves, as is the way. The wall is too bright for them: exposed to daylight, the photographs have given themselves up. Or else they escaped. The sun redeemed itself, claimed itself back, and took my parents with it.

The frame on the blue wall looks emptier each year. You can still, just about, make them out, but my mother and father are barely there, are barely here any more. My father left these rooms for an operation for cancer in August 1977, and he never came back. My mother died in my sister's house in 1994. She had grandchildren, he did not: he died six days before his first was born. Perhaps they remember him as an idea, or a man from their parents' stories, or even a man a stranger asks about (as happened me a couple of years ago when an elderly woman at a reading asked if I were his daughter, because he'd been kind to her once, she told me, and I nearly kissed her hand).

I barely knew my own grandparents, two of them having died well before I was born. I have few enough stories of them, some my mother told me about her mother, about growing up in New York. (Summers in the Catskills, daytrips to Rockaway Beach. Seeing *King Kong* with her father. Her mother distraught at Valentino's funeral. The Crash. An uncle's bathtub of hooch. Sailing home on the *Scythia*. She had good stories, my mother. I think they were her best company, these stories in frames of her telling, that she wrapped up nicely to give as gifts.) My father talked his past much less. His parents were dead by the time he was thirty-seven. We're not long livers on his side. Both my own parents were dead by the time I was thirty, my father having died when I was twelve.

If I'm honest these fading prints seem honest to me. The frames hold steady but what they frame becomes less certain, year on year. Sometime, someone younger than I will ask of them, what used to be here? And the photograph will likely be replaced by other photographs of who knows who, of one of us or some of us, sitting on a rock in sunshine, it being summer and life being softer and us having time on our hands. And so we will take our parents' places on the wall, looking into the room they looked into till they didn't, smiling for the good of it, out of the same frames.

My stay in the west of Ireland shuts up shop. Soon I will take the ferry to Manchester, me and the dog on the slow, early boat, then over and up from Holyhead. For a stretch of months, when I use the word *home*, I won't mean here. I will be Irish in England and this will mean, simultaneously, every-thing and nothing much. After nine years I think I have the measure of it. I suppose I live like the child I was, a sheet of tracing paper over a page, my dark head bent over intently while I make a copy true as I can with a blunt pencil in my hand. Instead of the bay there will be traffic on the Mancunian Way, a full tide of it morning and evening and, all night, the sound of it lapping my skylights; occasionally a blue siren to shred the silence of the room. Instead of Spiddal there will be Manchester, a coffee shop where they serve me a weak latté and never know my name. Instead of a turf fire there will be the electric one left with the flat, with a switch that throws a cheap flame show and the same patchy, overrated heat. In-stead of Lyric FM will be Radio 3, too much Rossini turning into too much John Tavener. Instead of a blue room will be a white room with a photo of the blue room on the wall. Instead of the rasp of a door handle that's made that sound for fifty years will be the ways of a place I am still getting used to; working out, as my blind dog does her route to the door, my progress through its rooms. Instead of the smell of bracken and fern will be heather-scented air freshener the cleaner sprays in the communal corridors each day.

My English life will frame my Irishness. In many ways it's a gentle enough frame that knows the size and shape cut for it and how to fill it without too much trumpetry or too little zeal. It's not a bad fit, though sometimes it feels slightly like wearing high heels to a kid's football game, or a hoodie to a job interview. Mostly I think I pass muster, vaguely at home in either place and maybe, at this stage, entirely in none. In one place I can be relied on to miss something of the other. But if the bay teaches anything about colour it's that, if you put two blues up against each other, they might chafe or flinch the way kids after school might cross the street when they see the same uniform. Two blues. And two sides to the street, all sides to the frame; one life in the middle, breathing in and out, like a sea scurrying between high and low tides whilst straddling its two shores.

This morning, with snow on the hills of Clare, light is a wash of silver on the bay. Last night, under a full moon, there was more gold to it. Is a day framed by two nights, or a night by two days, these days?

In the chalet I spend my days in the blue room. I nurse the fire and read and watch the sun sidle from the window on the left, near Ballyvaughan, to the Aran Islands, out to the right. That is how time passes here in January: in centimetres of glass, overlooking Galway Bay. It might rain or it might not. I might need supplies. I might go for a brown walk, or a brown and grey walk, down to the rocks through the boreen. I drink tea. I have no internet and no TV: little by little I go whole hours without the radio. I have received one text message in the past four days and that's fine by me. It's as if my life, my real life that has work and friends and schedules and duties, is blown like smoke from my turf fire over the wall and up the hill, to be lost in scrubland or to bolster cloud, to be nothing much to me. It's as if I have stepped out of a frame I've been putting in place around me now for years. I think of it: my flat, my job, the coffee I won't buy this Saturday, the paper I won't read. Nothing will fill my particular place unless it is the same sun I am watching now behind the hills of Clare. I am not there, I am here, in a frame of blue that doesn't belong to me or to anyone and that hasn't been made with any purpose in mind and has no business to do. A frame that is, first and foremost, about itself, and will continue to be regardless of whatever lives occupy it now and then. I slot in and when I leave I will slot out again, taking my markings, my kit and caboodle, all away with me.

And yet I'm not sure I have ever inhabited a room more completely. In sitting quietly for so many hours, in breathing silence, in waking to days which nothing will cram, in listening to waves and the road's plainsong, in having the fire sing me to sleep, I feel as if I intensify, somehow, and become more me. And all the lives I have lived so far, all the people I have loved or thought I might, all the quarrel I might have had with how things are or how things will be, all the minute calibrations of failure or success, all the wishing and desiring, all the plans and tallies, all the sorrows and songs, none of it counts for anything at all.

There is only the blue room and its cube of stillness, its perch over the bay. I inhabit it for a short time only and when I pull the door behind me it will not remember me. The only movement will be the shadow of a scatter of birds or the moon's silky sweet-talk on the back wall of the room. Until other lives come clattering through the door with their duvets and DVDs, lives that leave most of themselves elsewhere, that slip gently into this blue frame and fill it faithfully and wholeheartedly, for a while.

The ditch is the field's frame. The Lawn was the name of the field where we cut hay when I was a girl — I don't know why we didn't call it The Meadow as most folk would have done. Anyway, the Lawn was framed on three sides by ditches, one backing onto the road. All three, come spring, were cow-slips and primroses, still my favourite flowers. On the fourth was a cottage with a kitchen garden where the rhubarb, famous as far away as Athlone, thrived. That garden had its own frame, high ditches coming down with daffodils and peonies and lilac and foxgloves, while what was inside the frame was a working garden, where potatoes and vegetables and rhubarb and sweet apples turned, at various seasons, to hard cash. There the frame was ornament and what was framed was business, the business of keeping afloat, of getting through the year. The frame was for pleasure, the flowers grew wild, seeded themselves, required no husbandry, no work. But what the frame contained was all work and not easy work at that, digging, tending and harvesting; bending and straightening. Perhaps the flowers provided sensual relief from the soreness of the work. As I write a jug of white roses is in front of me. I like them for their correctness, their way of marshalling all the light in the room to attend on them. When the last ones died I replaced them with another bunch exactly the same; it seemed only courteous. A man I knew once praised me for bringing flowers in the house. He didn't care which flowers, but when I put pretty whitethorn in a vase one May my mother threw it straight back out and prayed to God my foolishness wouldn't result in bad luck. She knew the difference between indoors and out and knew the folly of breaching the divide. She had a point. Wood makes an excellent frame, but painting directly onto it is a tricky business, the wood being in thrall to its two dimensions and not a bit interested, when it comes down to it, in pretending to offer more. Keep wood for frames, keep flowers for ditches: let ornament know what it's up against. Let it handle itself carefully.

My young day belongs in a clip-frame: a frame without a frame. As a student, in a flat of my own, the walls were deco-rated almost exclusively with postcards in clip-frames. They were cheap, unpretentious and easily swopped round. So why have them at all, my old self wonders — why not just blu-tack postcards to the wall? Clip-frames were a nod in the direction of being grown up: a someway gesture between adult trappings and transitory student life. They weren't a big decision, just a glancing tribute to a possible future in which one would have real art in real frames, a real life to hang them in.

I graduated from postcards to posters: the clip-frames got bigger, more extravagant. But large clip-frames, at least in those days, were inclined to warp. It was like looking to the bottom of a swimming pool in winter, through fractious water and sweeps of wind. Nothing quite looked itself. And then I fell in love. We moved into a basement flat on Dublin's north side and set about setting up home. We bought cups that matched. We bought cheap bookshelves and painted them brightly, grew herbs on the windowsill. (As if we could press back a cold future with geegaws and salt cellars. But we were, more than anything, young.) We bought a blue mirror, set up two pine tables for writing desks, bought a rickety old green sofa and a couple of recipe books. We found that in trying to play house we'd made the place our own. Clearly our home, for such it was, would need pictures too, something including but so much more than the bits we'd gathered separately. And they would need frames, nothing flimsy or provisional, proper frames, solid frames, serious frames with real intent: they had a point to prove.

In those early days every frame I bought was either plain pine or else black. I still have a couple of them, earnest, thin things that have withstood the impulse to be lost along with so much else. I never buy frames like them any more: they are too puritan for me. Now it is all play I'm after, colour and joust, the unlikely association of what shouldn't suit. Now I want to be surprised; I don't want to make establishing gestures. I've had enough of them.

Though designed to protect frames are fragile in themselves. Like any wood they burn. We'd been young together, two poets making a world for ourselves, against all odds. (I want to write 'every odd', but an odd is an oxymoron, it seems: there has to be more than one of it, it requires at least one other companion, one answering parallel.) Poems and the writing of them were our high ground and, in the end, were our undoing. And yet. Though it was often tricky and money was an issue and making a living a finely tuned balancing act, I believed we were in it together. And we were. Until we were not. The night when another woman was mentioned did our family, the four of us, suddenly become three? Or did the four re-group itself in a different composition, two groups of three: one with me and our two kids; one with him and them? And she, the other woman, where would she fit in? Were there now seven sides to our family? (Have you ever seen a seven-sided frame? Or a five-sided one, for that matter?) So what did it do, this little frame? It did what any of us would have done: tossed around and contested, pulled every which way and that, subjected to so many question marks, it upped sticks and disappeared.

Break any frame down, what you're left with is a pile of sticks. Sticker. Stick insect. Sticky-fingered. Walking stick. Rain stick. The short end of the stick. The wrong end of the stick. Stick to it. Stick at it. Stick up for. Stick in the mind. Stick around. Stick in the mud. Stick to the point. Stick by your man. Stick in your craw. Stick it out. Stick to your guns. Stick to your story. Stick your neck out. Stick together. Stick with it. Be stuck with. Be stuck for. Be stuck on. Come unstuck.

And then you start building again. Corner to corner, edge to edge, you can't help yourself. And here I am. Not at all where I thought I'd be, in prose, conjecturally, but a true likeness (or maybe a true-enough likeness) all the same. Not that long since I looked about me and thought, where did everyone go? The frame seemed too empty without my sometime husband and my grown-up kids. So I made a smaller one and looked to words to fix me there, as they have always done. I construct a frame of words and I take up a position. This is me. This is one me. I hope there will be others yet, and different frames to house them in, flightier maybe, less solid, and less absolute than this.

'Surely the use of the first person was a mistake.'
— *Manchester Guardian* review of Janet Frame's
*Faces In The Water* (1961)

A frame comes between an object and the function it once had. How to make an object useless? Stick it in a frame.

Being in the middle of something requires that there somewhere be a perimeter, an edge. I am middle-aged, the world and its insurance categories tell me. But what is it I am in the middle of, and where should I look for this edge? Any life has two edges, two ends, the start and end points, birth and death. That it isn't a numbers game for us to call is evident from the baggy, loose-waisted term 'middle age'. The term shirks its own responsibilities: it's not sure, I suspect, what it's supposed to mean. Nobody can identify the very point where they are, in fact, middle-aged, unless with the benefit of time-travel or Godlike insight and, even then, they'd better think fast in the nanosecond left to reckon the hour of their dying and the backward mathematical computations involved in locating the halfway point. Some people will be middle-aged at twenty-two; some people at two days. Right now, beyond the edges of these words, some person is entering the eye of his or her middle age, innocently and carelessly. I am almost certainly past mine. If my parents' lives are anything to go by, I likely passed over the point of my mid-life some fifteen years ago at a moment when the Life Assurance ready reckoner still had me pegged as a bankable risk, which someone might also call young.

Only one edge is fixed and knowable to us: mine occurred at 4.20 am on Monday, October 19th, 1964, my mother wrote it in her diary. Its companion bookend will be set down in yet another hand. Whatever I write in my own hand in between seems comparatively insignificant. Meanwhile I can think of myself as middle-aged at fifty-one, or as middle-aged at no time. In theory, anyway. You'd need to be brazen for the latter. You'd need your magic shield about you to repel the claptrap of the body cutting up rough and the clatter of the mind chasing itself down, and the pockmarked future that you try to stuff with the stuff to hand, the holidays and hairdos and daydreams and plans. You need your magic shield about you to cut through the knots your life ties itself in, none of them particularly ingenious or to be relied upon. And you'll need your magic sword to cut a wee hole in the burlap of invisibility the world thinks it OK to throw over our heads. Because it's important to be able to see out now and then. It's important to have range.

Birth and death, yeah, yeah, yeah. Even the thinnest connecting line has more than an end and a beginning: it must also have a top and a bottom, if it is a physical thing. So what might the other two edges of my life be? The highs and lows. The ups and downs. The public and private. The give and take. The live and let live. Innocence and experience. Silence and noise. Love and loss. Together and alone.

My birth, my death, my opposite meanings as held in the same breath: perhaps these are the edges of the age I am in the middle of. Between the I and the Not I (the same line in both directions) I am middling. I am centred. I am framed.

> What immortal hand or eye
> Could frame thy fearful symmetry?
> — William Blake, 'The Tyger'

Four sides full (like the three bags of the nursery rhyme). Four sides of the frame to keep me steady in the here and now. Any one of three sides could wither and I'd be safe enough, but not the bottom of the frame, the horizontal, lined up to earth and sky, the ground beneath my feet. Without it I fear I would fall and fall and never climb back up. But with it in place I know where I ought to be. I have the measure of me.

> As if my life were shaven,
> And fitted to a frame . . .
> > — Emily Dickinson,
> > 'It Was Not Death, for I Stood Up'

Times, the frame of my body seems like no kind of frame at all. It desires nothing more than to squander itself and all its limits and distinctions. What it wants is to feel at one with the world, to be not alone in itself. But it serves, at least, to keep the surrealist mechanics of my guts and organs in place, where I need them to be, so that the part of me that is flightier is free to roam as any ghost on a moor, to call at any window. And it will. It ranges and dips and swirls, does it ever, and I am tethered to it, this creature of fantasy, until I grow heartily sick and tired of so much desire.

I want my frame to settle for the frame it needs to be: serviceable, a little prone to crack and splinter, an unbending, dogged thing. I have no use at the age I am for a frame that magics itself, night after night, around other scenarios, unlived lives, possibilities. I need it here for company. I need it to be sure I am still here, at a fixed point of loneliness, balanced and secure.

Do I exist, if I live alone, at the centre of my life? Surely that would involve comings and goings, lines of distraction, clamour and event which I must hold together, busy tightrope act? We are mostly fixed in place by the frame of other people's needs and I am the still point of a turning world, I reckon, only if the world is turning: otherwise we are in collapse. The lack of routine, or at least the lack of other people's routines, the long hours in which nobody asks anything of me, these might as well be my life and, being new to me, I am still exploring them, still feeling my way in relative dark, not occupying it firmly or with any authority. I still find myself constantly expecting this life to disappear. Let the front door open, my name be called, let a question be asked of me. Let me find words to make up an answer, so I might hear myself respond. Let me be pulled, again, hither and yon, so that I need to stand still for a moment or two, get my bearings, sift through all these requirements, these duties, to know my place and to cleave to it, to work outwards from there.

It has been a lovely evening, a group of us sat around a table in the house of friends. Early summer and the light is testing its recent, hesitant decision to commit. The high tree at the end of the garden seems to establish a darkness against which the dribs and drabs of light flutter and stall. The children bring torches outside; we watch from the back door as they daub inscrutable symbols over a fledgling dark. And then the taxi is waiting. Behind me is everyone in the bright hall, gathering children and distributing coats, stuffing limbs into busy lives. I step into the dark. I remember this darkness from being a child, how I'd run, always a little too frantically, from the car to the front door coming home at night. It was too big for me, that darkness, too full. The only protection against it was the front door closing just in time before it nuzzled its way into the hall and turned on us, all snarl and claws. Here in this city it seems tamer but I know that is an act. Between the door of my friends' house and the taxi it snaps at my ankles and tugs on my coat. I am the only single person here, the odd number that's easy for darkness to corner and pick off once I step out of the frame. The house is the frame, and my friends are the frame, and so is the sound of their lives as I climb in the taxi and go home alone. 'Nice evening?' asks the taxi driver. 'Lovely,' I say as I pull my coat around me and feel for holes sharp teeth have made, count scratches on my skin. It has not forgotten me, the darkness; it waits with infinite patience, knowing that one of these times when I can't pull the door quite fast enough, when I am stranded in solitude and most small and frightened, it will get me, nothing surer, and make bits of me.

And sometimes, winter evenings with the light drawing in, I wonder what it would be like if there were no life, no frame, to be the centre of.

What will the world do when I am dead? I could weep for its loss, the loss of me, except I couldn't really, not without irony.

Other people die all the time, but that's different. They're not me.

There I am, out in the yard, an unhinged, short-arsed marionette, stomping my foot and punching the air. I can see me from my bedroom window up in the gods. But the yard, the air, and especially death, they've a mind to laugh at me.

'You come to this place, mid-life. You don't know how you got there, but suddenly you're staring fifty in the face. When you turn and look back down the years, you glimpse the ghosts of other lives you might have led. All your houses are haunted by the person you might have been.'
— Hilary Mantel, *Giving Up the Ghost* (2004)

I may have grown superstitious since I came to live alone. Superstitious is the name I give it, to fend off other names. What are they, these barely shadows I almost see in the hallway? Flits of light and flaps of cold that open for a second and then seal up again. But what should I call it when someone dead these forty years sits beside me on the grey couch? To give it a name is to make a space for it in the already jumbled surface of things. Slap language on what has no need of a word, you can't unfix it again. I have explanations, of course; they are easily come by. They range from the logical to the psychological, from tricks of the light to ways of conjuring homely company. I live in a converted mill built in the 1830s when Manchester's industrial revolution was spinning dizzily. Typically, a mill worker worked fourteen hours a day. One third of mill workers were children, the youngest of whom were 'scavengers', whose job was to crawl underneath machinery in motion to gather loose bits of cotton. Fatal accidents were commonplace. Life expectancy for a labourer in 1840s' Manchester was twenty-four.[xxxiv] Home, when they went there, was likely to be a damp cellar with no ventilation, no sanitation and no running water. Diarrhoea was the main cause of infant mortality. Mill fever (aching limbs and headache) was common, as were tuberculosis, bronchitis and asthma, on account of the amount of cotton lint and dust in the air. Little Ireland (described by Friedrich Engels in his *Description of the Working Class in England in 1844* as a 'horrid little slum') is directly behind my street, marked by a red plaque. These were my people, escaping here from (presumably) even worse conditions at home.

Roll back. Imagine. The room where I type is full of looms and women. The noise is deafening. Even when the machines knock off for the day it will take a while to be able to distinguish any Irish accents here. But here they must be. And here she is by a trick of the pen, a woman standing in her pinny and laced-up boots, tired beyond exhaustion. She looks up at the same roof beams as I do, could steady herself by the same wall. Imagine the air shifts, realigns, and she can somehow see me, one woman owning this room and three others, one middle-aged woman, healthy as a pineapple, with a job that won't kill me, able to wake to the knowledge that, unless I am very unlucky, no one will hurt me this day.

I am a poet: I believe the surface of my life is pretty much wafer-thin. What matters (if it matters) is not the business of the this-and-that, but something that rises (by stealth or magic) from stillness and silence. I can't seem to stop myself believing that sequence and structure, the logical ordering of a time-sodden world, is so much stuff and nonsense. In deploying metaphor and simile I ply lines of connection that have to be both plausible and surprising. I have to dig for them: if they present themselves too easily chances are they're ready-made. So I look for lines of connection between what is not obviously connected (and if sometimes I trip over those lines, then so be it). Buried lines, staggered lines, lines that stutter and disappear — they are a poet's stock-in-trade, the network that supports a poem, that holds the thing intact. Here is one. It is not implausible to me that if I can imagine — for better or worse — one moment of another woman's life, that she might also imagine mine. Not in every detail of course but in terms of an essential freedom that might correct the essential, woeful circumstances of her life. And that act of imagining puts her here where I am now, having conjured her into the frame of the present, into the frame of this room, where she is now a presence, scantly reconnoitred, barely shadow, flit of light and flap of cold.

Sinyavsky again: 'I walk about the house like a ghost. Not the ghost that lived here in the past. But the one that is yet to come.'[xxxv]

Louis van Tilborgh writes about the framing of Van Gogh: 'There were almost as many new frames as new owners, for it is unusual for the frame to be retained when a picture changes hands. It is the only part of a painting that a new owner can alter in order to make an acquisition truly his own.'[xxxvi] I suspect this is how we live our lives, in a sequence of frames either of our own or of another's desiring. Married, I lived in one kind of frame; single, I live in another. This is how I present myself to the world. I can't describe it, exactly, this frame (but I don't think it has much truck with gilt). The description would be another frame and then I would have to, of course, take a look at that. On it would go, a mirror sequence, frame after frame, a moving picture that moves nothing at all. Maybe the frame always tells the story of itself in the end — of its past and future, its fiction and facts — and isn't all that interested in what the picture has to say. Maybe the truest frames would frame the back of the canvas, not the front. Maybe the truest frames frame nothing, thereby becoming splendid gestures of their own integrity and self-centredness.

Perhaps that is what happens when a marriage ends: the frame dismantles and all that is left is for the couple to step over the little pile of shavings and dust that was their together life, and slip off by separate exits, leaving a blanked-out space on a wall, outlined in patchy dark.

After a break-up, who gets custody of the family photo-graphs? You'll probably have creative ideas about what to do with those photos of your partner taken by you years ago. You might leave family photographs up on the wall, but take down those of the two of you. (You'll probably notice what a strange phrase that is — *the two of you*.) You could reuse the frames for other photos that won't have him or her in them. Or else, don't. Put them, frame and photo both, in tight-lipped storage boxes you can't see into; then stow them for maybe years and years in some dark and harmless place.

Would the Me I write in language recognize the Me I live? Cornelia Parker's 'Self-portrait as a Square' (part of a series usually exhibited together and titled 'Self-portrait as a Square / Circle / Line / Triangle')[xxxvii] looks like a red square framing a blank space, surrounded in turn by more blank space. The white, wooden frame around it follows faithfully the shape of the square, so that two sets of lines make three demarcated areas: the centre of the square, the area between square and frame and, ultimately, the frame. What is extraordinary about this vivid square is that it is drawn in the artist's blood: she has literally made her life blood into a work of art. This perhaps is the truest and most fearless autobiography, but to do likewise would require me to draw enough blood from my own self to use as ink for handwriting every one of these letters and words. I reckon that would be more than a body's worth, even over time. Were I to adopt this practice I would have to write much less. Or else, I suppose, I could select certain passages to be red-letter text. But that would give too much away: like putting some phrases in a different font and into bold and larger type, it would blare significance and shout down any other writing in plain ink with no prior knowledge of my life, except what I presently assign. I write in innocence: nothing about these words knows more about me than I tell them to. The ink has its own history. So does my laptop. So does the typeface. So do the words. But I am only a glance against these timelines: I am where they meet now. Perhaps these words relate to my life as Parker's frames relate to her drawn blood — they follow faithfully its lineation, but they are made of sterner stuff. (Logically, if squeamishly, a full self-portrait in this vein would involve a frame made of her bone, and paper derived from her skin. I have no equivalents. My self-portrait is only suggestive, and though I have put myself into these words, they are, in no way, literally me.)

Putting mirrors into frames is comical, when you think of it, like pretending that what's to be seen there is a work of art. As I write an oval mirror in a gold frame high on the wall opposite me gives a piece of sky back to the whole. The sky doesn't seem to care especially for the gift. It has other business in hand and no need to make bits of itself.

'This great world . . . is the mirror in which we must look at ourselves to recognize ourselves from the proper angle.'
— Michel de Montaigne[xxxviii]

Home Depot sells a Montaigne Mirror. The website describes its weathered oak frame in naturally finished wood and wonderful design details. 'Place it in your bath (sic) for a clean, transitional look. Not magnifying. Not fog free. Assembly required.'

I would like to write poems with mirror sequins stitched to them where the words should be. Or, failing that, I would like to write blanked-out poems, a book with not a single word in it, just blocks of black, redacted text surrounded by fascinating frames of white that do the poems' heavy lifting for them, and tell all there is to tell.

Or, if I lost my nerve, I could make each poem look like a Sappho poem, all fits and starts, words unpicking, undoing themselves almost as quickly and as determinedly as they were put into place. It would be like framing positives alongside negatives, except the two do not line up. It would be like a befuddling crossword puzzle with no answers, or rather

97

with a thousand answers, none of which quite fits. It could be construed as an invitation: I give you a fraction of the words and you come up with the rest. Stand beside me where I stand, watch it in construction, from my point of view. Or would you prefer to stand in front of the finished thing and look at it head-on, as one does pictures in a gallery, safe and finished, inviolably framed? Do you want to help me lift the poem in and out of the hinged frame that opens towards you, or do you prefer the kind of frame that brooks no interference, that will not be opened or closed?

A certain kind of frame exaggerates its contents. It picks up on a colour or a tone and, by repeating it in a different context, emphasizes it. Klimt and Stuck used shimmering frames of worked silver or sheet copper, not quite Yeats's hammered gold and gold enamelling, but not far off either. The frames made icons of their artwork, turned the naked female body into a religious image, sanctified by context. Put a life in a frame of expensive material, it accrues significance, it can't help itself. I have chosen a black frame, the plainest I can find, but still I recognize the problem of having framed something not quite worthy of the frame. Think of it as a small portrait, a little darker than it needs to be, in the tradition, say, of a lesser Dutch school, a school in the sticks, that had a good instructor once, but it was years ago. I have put a woman in a black dress against a black background. Only her face is pale, and a collar of lace that sets it off. She is middle-aged, no beauty, but maybe there's something interesting in the way she looks out at the room. Let her be framed, so, in candour, in an impulsive truth. Of course it is a small portrait that won't want to make much of itself. So let us humour her. Put it in a shuttered corner where only shadows fall. And then let morning happen, as it has to do. See what the day makes of the thing, the way it squanders shadow so the portrait and the frame and all give up their clamorous darkness to the play of light. See what she does: she undoes herself in a mesh of brightness, and the going comes easy to her.

As a framer you work back from the glass. There is a frame into which glass fits. You lay it down, glass to the front and you position the artwork centred on a mount with tape. Then stiff backing, then nails or clips to secure it to the frame. Then tape for sealing it. Finally the means of hanging, screws into the frame and a piece of cord. You will have been checking now and then from the front to make sure it's straight and centred. Also, free from dust and smudge. But when you turn the framed artwork over it will look different, of course. It will look more definite, complete.

Believe me, says the painting.
Trust me, says the frame.

❖

In this room
four straight walls
position me perfectly.

❖

Between the solitude of a tree,
a clothes line and a fence post,
be careful where you stand.

❖

You at a desk wedged between mountains.
You with your head in the clouds.

❖

A beak so orange the day ignites.
By the time I get the camera on
there is only my shadow on the grass,
a day switched off again.

❖

What of the day with its locks and keys,
its many rusted hours?

❖

Birds between bars of a pinstripe curtain
make music of a wall.

❖

Clouds scrabble in behind trees.
A door closes. A bird stops singing.
Today shuts up shop.

❖

A figure in a dark room
removing its black coat.

❖

Trees in their white nightdresses.
Stones with their mouths agape.

❖

An ebony frame on a night-time scene:
where do I begin?

❖

Years on, I can still set my breath to it,
the black clock in the framed room.

# Four Painted Frames

### 1

Cue the chimney pots and railings.
Cue the asparagus fern.
Cue the skyline's thumbs-up to the sky.
Cue the window.
Cue the gold of the gold frame.
Cue the plump hour alone.
Cue the green dress embroidered with ships.
Cue the same love song.

### 2

If days are peaceable as a chastised child
nights shuttlecock old dreams.
If days rest timid on a rim of years
nights corner in black frames.
If days hold on to every rain
nights make tiny chains of words

and throw them, wildly,
up onto the moon.

### 3

I have painted, I realize, my nails
the colour of those railings which is
a colour of the sky behind rooflines
drawn like notes onto a stave.
The city sings them, practice scales,
through my open door. There is life.
I could put it in a yellow frame,
hang it where the mirror used to be.

One day, any day, it will sit where I sit,
try on my clothes, slip into my voice
and put itself about instead of me.
Where will I go then, what will I do?
I will compliment it in the mornings
and kiss its eyelids, sweetly, every night.


4

Ask me again in bright light,
I might know better then.

i

# Notes

[i]Henri Matisse, 'Témoignage', *Écrits et propos sur l'art* (Paris, Hermann, 1972), p.196

[ii]Edward Thomas, *Poems* (Holt, 1917)

[iii]Quoted in Paul Tingen, *Miles Beyond* (New York, Billboard Books, 2001), Chapter 1

[iv]Vincent van Gogh, letter to his brother, Theo, October 8, 1888. *The Complete Letters of Vincent van Gogh*, Robert Harrison (ed) (Boston, Bulfinch, 2000), No. 547

[v]Edgar Degas, quoted in Peter Brunette & David Wills (eds), *The Spatial Arts* (Cambridge, CUP, 1994), p.120

[vi]Quoted in Jacob Simon, *The Art of the Picture Frame* (London, National Portrait Gallery, 1998), p.86

[vii]Hugh Brigstocke, *William Buchanan and the Nineteenth Century Art Trade* (New Haven, CT, Paul Mellon Centre for Studies in British Art, 1982), p.181

[viii]Sarah Uwins, *A Memoir of Thomas Uwins* RA (London, Longman & Brown, 1858) vol 2, p.131

[ix]Helena Hayward and Pat Kirkham, *William and John Linnell: 18th Century London Furniture Makers* (London, Studio Vista — Christies, 1980), p.45

[x]Jacob Simon, *ibid* (1998), p.142

[xi]Information for this section relies on Chapter 6, 'Framemakers and the Business of Framemaking' in Jacob Simon, *ibid* (1998), pp.129-148

[xii]Quoted in *Arts and Aesthetics in a Globalising World*, Raminder Kaur and Parul Dave-Mukherji (eds) (London, Bloomsbury, 2014), p. 74

[xiii]C K Chesterton, *Orthodoxy* (London, The Bodley Head, 1908), p.32

[xiv]Charles Eastlake, *Hints on Household Taste in Furniture, Upholstery and Other Details* (London, Longmans, Green & Co, 1869)

[xv]Gertrude Stein, 'Pictures', *Lectures in America* (New York, Random House, 1935), p.57

[xvi]Whistler to George Lucas, quoted in Caroline Doswell Older's *American Artists' Frames* (PhD Thesis, University of California, Santa Barbara, 2007), p.32

[xvii]*ibid*

[xviii]José Ortega y Gasset, 'Meditations on the Frame', translated by Andrea L Bell in *Perspecta* (1990), vol 26, pp.185-190

[xix]Piet Mondrian (1943) quoted in Yve-Alain Bois, *Painting as Model* (October Books, 1993), p.171

[xx]Metropolitan Museum of Art Catalogue entry: www.metmuseum.org/toah/works-of-art/C.I.69.23

[xxi]Seamus Heaney, interview with Rand Brandes, *Salmagundi* (Issue 80, Fall 1988), pp.4-21

[xxii]Jean-Claude Lebensztejn, 'Starting out from the frame: vignettes', Brunette & Wills (eds), *Deconstruction and the Visual Arts* (Cambridge, CUP, 1994), pp.118-40

[xxiii]*Exchanging Hats: Elizabeth Bishop, Paintings*, William Benton (ed), (Manchester, Carcanet, 1997), p.67

[xxiv]Andrey Sinyavsky, *A Voice from the Chorus* (London, Collins & Harvill, 1975), p. 203

[xxv]*ibid*, p. 204

[xxvi]*ibid*, p.279

[xxvii]Robert Motherwell's Introduction to *Joseph Cornell's Theatre of the Mind: Selected Diaries, Letters and Files* (London, Thames and Hudson, 1994)

[xxviii]Diana Souhami, *Gluck* (London, Pandora, 1988), p.103

[xxix]Quoted in Jacob Simon, *ibid* (1998), p.185

[xxx]Souhami, *ibid* (1988), p.104

[xxxi]Souhami, *ibid* (1988), p. 229

[xxxii]William Shakespeare, *Coriolanus*, Act V, Scene iii

[xxxiii]Alasdair Maclean, *Night Falls on Ardnamurchan* (Edinburgh, Birlinn, 2001), p.163

[xxxiv]Mark Nathan Cohen, *Health and the Rise of Civilisation*, (New Haven, Yale University Press, 1989), p.202

[xxxv]Andrey Sinyavsky, *ibid* (1975), p. 319

[xxxvi]Louis van Tilborgh, 'Framing Van Gogh 1880-1990', *In Perfect Harmony: Picture and Frame 1850-1920*, Eva Mendgen, (ed), (Amsterdam, Van Gogh Museum, 1995), pp.163-182

[xxxvii]Cornelia Parker, 'Self-portrait as a Square / Circle / Line / Triangle', 2015. Blood and pencil (63x63cm). The Whitworth Art Gallery, Manchester.

[xxxviii]Michel de Montaigne, *The Complete Works: Essays, Travel Journal, Letters*, translated by Donald M Frame (London, Everyman's Library, 2003), *ii*.11. p.141

The historical information in this essay draws on the following sources:

Henry Heydenryk, *The Art and History of Frames* (London, Nicholas Vane, 1964)

Eva Mendgen (ed), *In Perfect Harmony: Picture and Frame 1850-1920* (Amsterdam, Van Gogh Museum, 1995)

Paul Mitchell and Lynn Roberts, *A History of European Picture Frames* (London, Merrell Holberton, 1996)

Paul Mitchell and Lynn Roberts, *Frameworks: Form, Function and Ornament in European Portrait Frames* (London, Merrell Holberton, 1996)

Jacob Simon, *The Art of the Picture Frame* (London, National Portrait Gallery, 1998)

C000146093

# The Real Food

# Cook Book

*Nutritious & delicious dishes for*

*the whole family to enjoy*

**Ellen Picton**

**Zoë Harcombe**

Published by Columbus Publishing Ltd 2016
www.columbuspublishing.co.uk

ISBN 978-1-907797-69-9
Version 20190904

Copyright @ 2016 Ellen Picton

Ellen Picton has asserted her right to be identified as the author of this work in accordance with the Copyright, Designs and Patents Act 1988.

All rights reserved. No part of this publication may be reproduced, stored in retrieval system, or transmitted in any form or by any means, electronic, mechanical, photocopying or otherwise without the prior permission of the author.

A CIP record of this book is available from the British Library.

Cover design by Andy Harcombe

Typesetting and design by Raffaele Bolelli Gallevi

All photography copyright © James Knight 2016

Brand and product names are trademarks or registered trademarks of their respective owners.

The content of this book is intended to inform, entertain and provoke your thinking. This is not intended as medical advice. It may, however, make you question current medical and nutritional advice. That's your choice. It's your life and health in your hands.

Neither the author nor the publisher can be held responsible or liable for any loss or claim arising from the use, or misuse, of the content of this book.

# Acknowledgements

I must start by thanking Zoë and Andy Harcombe for supporting this project, without them this book would not be possible.

I am dedicating this book to my Grandfather, Ceri Parry, who always gave me words of wisdom and encouragement. He gave me many recipe books and wrote messages in each. My favourite says: 'To the queen of cuisine on your 17th birthday, keep cooking – good looking'. And so I did.

I must thank my husband, Anthony, for all his support, for listening to all of my recipe ideas, and for giving feedback on new dishes but most importantly, for cleaning the pans that don't fit in the dishwasher.

I hope that when my daughter, Isabelle, is older she will love cooking as I do.

*Ellen Picton*

# Contents

# Introduction
# (By Zoë)

Ellen is an incredible person with an incredible personal health story. Aged 19, she was diagnosed with Coeliac disease. The prescription for gluten-free (fake) foods stimulated Ellen's interested in nutrition and real food for two reasons i) because the gluten-free fabrications made her feel so unwell and ii) because they tasted so bad!

Ellen's next health diagnosis was even more upsetting and potentially life changing: in her early 20s she started to suffer with disabling endometriosis. She spent most days strapped to a tens machine and was downing a cocktail of anti-inflammatory drugs in tandem. After several operations, which tried to resolve the endometriosis, Ellen was given the unimaginable choice of having a hysterectomy or being put on a drug to induce the menopause. She was only 24 years old. Ellen was told that she couldn't have children due to the extent of the scar tissue in her womb. Having just met her now husband, Anthony, she had to break the news to him that children wouldn't be part of the package. Thankfully he thought that Ellen was more than enough ☺

While still in shock at the no-children news, Ellen declined both stark medical choices (hysterectomy or menopause) and set out to see how healthy she could become with lifestyle changes. She tried to optimise her nutrition intake, dropped full time work to part time, took up yoga and enjoyed daily walks. Within six weeks of starting the 'healthy-me plan', Ellen then enjoyed the shock of her life – a pregnancy!

The doctors were equally shocked and were convinced that the baby wouldn't make it to term. But "Isabelle" liked being inside Ellen so much, she arrived two week's late. A perfect, healthy baby – or, as Ellen and Anthony describe her "their miracle baby".

Following Isabelle's arrival, Ellen knew that her heart and calling lay in food and nutrition. She took a diploma in nutrition and set up her company "Healthaspire" in Milford Haven Marina – a more natural and inspirational setting would be difficult to find. The premises have a fully accredited cooking demonstration and education facility and two consultation rooms for private consultations.

Ellen was introduced to The Harcombe Diet® by a friend, who had lost weight and managed her own endometriosis by following the plan. Ellen tried the five day Phase 1 and felt great and wished she'd discovered me sooner to avoid years of unnecessary yo-yo dieting (I wish I'd discovered it sooner for the same reason! But then I'd never know what everyone is going through...)

Ellen was looking for a real food, healthy eating plan to adopt at "Healthaspire" and was keen to see if The Harcombe Diet® could be shared in this way. She thought the company was American and so was delighted to hear another Welsh voice at the end of the phone when she tracked us down and spoke to my husband, Andy. We were exploring the possibility of running local clubs at the time and so we were delighted to have the opportunity to help Ellen to run some sessions, to see how the concept would work. The local results were amazing: most people lost 30lbs (15kg) and cured so many ailments alongside.

Ellen has been running weekly groups since January 2015 and has seen hundreds of members lose amazing amounts of weight. She makes the classes unique by discussing a new nutrition topic at each one, or doing a cooking demonstration. Ellen also offers 1-1 private weight loss coaching for people who want something more personal and Skype sessions too, for those further away – even Spain! Ellen is pleased to observe that The Harcombe Diet® delivers what it promises, which is to 'Lose weight and Gain health!'

I have personally presented in Ellen's demonstration room to her club members, with the sun setting over the sea and the seagulls squawking all around. After the talk, over drinks and Harcombe friendly nibbles, I've heard so many wonderful success stories from the regulars: life changing weight loss; diabetes under control and all sorts of digestive problems resolved with real food and Ellen's help.

On one occasion, Ellen hired the local theatre, so that 100 real foodies could come along to hear me speak and sample Ellen's tasty recipes.

It is not an overstatement to say that Ellen is, pretty much single handed, making a difference to the health of Pembrokeshire. In addition to the local clubs, Ellen runs cooking lessons for adults and children, to help them to prepare simple meals from scratch. She has been invited to do cooking demonstrations at food and fish festivals – well, Pembrokeshire is known for the latter! Such is the enthusiasm that Ellen has for cooking and such is the impact that her sessions have, Milford Fish Docks, part of the Port of Milford Haven, have generously sponsored numerous local children to attend cookery courses. Ellen's demonstration record is teaching 140 children to make tuna paté and healthy chocolate treats at a local food festival.

A local private school approached Ellen to ask for help with their school menu and Ellen inspired them to go for a 'refined sugar-free' meal plan. The parents and teachers have been as important as the school chef in achieving this stretch target. The parents and teachers are the ones who should benefit from better behaviour and concentration from the 'stable energy' children. Ellen is now a master at hiding vegetables in everyday foods, although children are more inclined to like sweet carrots etc anyway, when they don't have artificial sweetness in their diet.

Healthy eating really has changed Ellen's life and may have played a part in creating another life – Isabelle! It's now her vocation, her passion and her way of keeping her own health conditions under control. Her joy at helping others to be slimmer and healthier is clear to see. This book is Ellen's way of sharing some of the dishes that she cooks – whether in the home kitchen, the business demo area or at food festivals. Enjoy!

*Dr. Zoë Harcombe, PhD*

# Why The Real Food Cook Book?
## (By Ellen)

The working title for this book was "Freefrom?", before we settled upon "The Real Food Cook Book." All the recipes are gluten-free and most are dairy-free and sugar-free. On the rare occasions that milk is used as an ingredient, other dairy-free options are suggested. Sugar, as in sucrose/table sugar, won't be listed anywhere (other than to look out for sugar in bought ingredients to avoid it!) However, there is some sucrose in the very dark chocolate used in some puddings and dried fruit features in a couple of desserts and honey/maple syrup in one. Hence, we won't claim that the whole book is dairy-free and sugar-free, but the majority of recipes are free from things that you may need/choose to avoid. This will be a great addition to your "Freefrom" recipe repertoire, depending on what you and your family personally want to avoid.

When I was 19 I was diagnosed with Coeliac disease. Coeliac disease is an autoimmune condition. This is where the immune system mistakenly attacks healthy tissue. There is no real cure, apart from removing gluten from the diet.

At the time I was offered a prescription for gluten-free goods, but I did not want to eat all of the processed alternatives. I have always loved cooking, so I enjoyed the new challenge of recreating my favourite recipes to make them naturally gluten-free.

A few years later I became lactose intolerant, so again this meant I had to play around with alternative ideas. Discovering The Harcombe Diet®, I had to give up sugar too! I thought life without gluten, dairy and sugar would be hard. People often ask me, "What exactly do you eat?" This recipe book holds the answers and I hope it helps to inspire you as much as it has done me.

The Harcombe Diet® has helped me to maintain a weight loss of three stone and it has stopped me feeling the depths of despair of yo-yo dieting. It's perfect for me as it naturally excludes all the foods that cause me problems and fits alternatives into a lifestyle that I can live with and enjoy. It most certainly did what it promised, which was to help me to lose weight and gain health!

Food intolerance is becoming more common and many people are having problems, mainly with gluten, wheat and dairy. The 'Freefrom' sections in supermarkets are growing by the minute. The key issue is – just because it's gluten-free, doesn't mean it's healthy. The moral of the story is – eat real food.

These recipes help me to feel that I'm not deprived of anything. They make meals that I eat on a daily basis and they work for all of my family, which includes a hungry husband, an active four year old, and two dogs that eat real food too.

I dislike bland food and Freefrom food shouldn't mean you have to sacrifice on taste. This recipe book should give you lots of 'Freefrom' ideas, which are bursting full of flavour.

A large number of the recipes in this book are also Freefrom meat and fish and are therefore suitable for vegetarians. We've marked these with (V) in the title of each recipe.

*Ellen Picton*

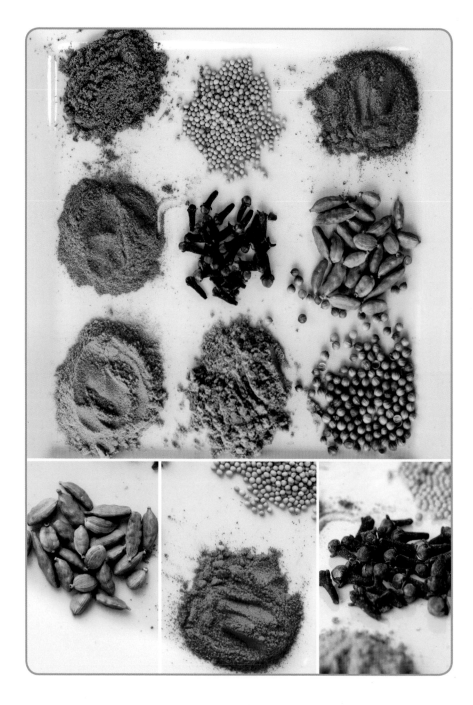

# Stocking Your Larder

Having a well stocked store cupboard in your kitchen really does help when you are trying to throw something together. At first it may seem expensive to buy all of these things, but once you have them they seem to last forever.

I have an entire cupboard and spice rack dedicated to flavour; I love how a few sprinkles of this and that can make such a huge difference to a dish.

### Herbs

Dried herbs are really helpful, my favourites include parsley, oregano and rosemary. If you do buy fresh herbs then put any leftovers in the freezer. Then, when you need them, you can crumble them into your cooking pot; they taste just as good as they would fresh.

> *Top tip – DO NOT throw away the stalks of coriander and parsley – this is a common kitchen mistake – all of the herb has flavour!*

### Spices

Unless you have a spice grinder, get ground spices. Garam masala is a really helpful one as it's a blend of Indian spices, which makes an instant curry powder. It usually doesn't contain chilli, so you can add flavour without heat.

Dried chilli powder, cumin and coriander, along with turmeric, are also on my spice rack. You can choose garlic powder too, although I must admit I'm a lover of fresh.

### Fats

Fat is absolutely essential for the human body. There are good and bad fats. Avoid sunflower and oils high in polyunsaturated fat. They are highly processed and not as healthy as they sound. Stick with cold pressed oils such as olive oil. Use an extra virgin olive oil for salad dressing and a cheaper version for frying.

Coconut oil has become very popular lately. It's really versatile and is naturally stable at high temperatures, making it ideal for frying, roasting, adding to soups or baking.

I also use coconut oil to take my make up off and as a moisturiser - just make sure you have one pot for the bathroom and one for the kitchen!

Butter, lard and beef dripping are also natural. One of my favourite side dishes is onions fried in beef dripping – try to make celeriac roasties with it, add some salt – and potatoes will soon be a thing of the past!

### Vinegar
Raw apple cider vinegar and balsamic are great for salad dressings.

### Stock Cubes
Check they don't contain wheat as many do, I tend to use a yeast-free stock powder.

Gluten-free soy sauce – Tamari – a little bit goes a long way

### Thickeners
Arrow root, corn flour or ground almonds are all good Freefrom substitutes.

### Red and White Wine
It's always worth having a bottle of red and white in the house, as there are a number of recipes that are really enhanced by wine. Red wine goes well with tomato, for example – as the French and Italians know well.

# Shopping for Real Food

Once you get into shopping for 'real food' then your supermarket visit is so much quicker, as there are only a few aisles that you need to visit.

Try to avoid Freefrom shelves in supermarkets, as they are highly processed. If you are tempted by something processed then read the ingredients and if you don't recognise something then don't eat it!

Here are my top tips for real food shopping:

## 1) Where possible – buy local
Most Fridays you will find my sausage dog Martha and I at the local Farmers' market. It's one of the highlights of the week. I love trying new produce and Martha gets lots of treats too.

By shopping locally it means you eat seasonally and you support the local economy too – win win all round!

## 2) Try something new
The great thing about buying local is that you are usually buying from the grower or producer themselves, so if there is something you are unsure of then ask.

You will usually get lots of ideas about how to cook or serve the dish.

## 3) Do you really need it?
I like to think if it's not for sale at the Farmers market then do I really need it?

You will usually find meats, fish, eggs, vegetables, fruit, salads, cheeses, cream, butter, milk and local honey, which is more than enough to stop you from going hungry.

## 4) Buy the best you can afford
Try to buy organic or outdoor bred meat, wild fish and free range eggs along with the most local and fresh vegetables you can get your hands on.

If you feel that eating this way is expensive then remind yourself how much a takeaway meal would be – plus your body is the only place you have to live, so it's worth the investment, after all – food is medicine!

### 5) Avoid temptation

If you are someone who is easily tempted by packets and marketing ploys then you can try to shop online. Also make sure you don't visit the supermarket when you are hungry.

# Tips to Make Cooking Fun and Easy

## 1) Bulk cook
Every time I cook I always make more than I need, then freeze some.

## 2) Music
Play your favourite tunes. If you don't like to cook this is a great way to pass the time.

## 3) Try something new
We all get stuck in a rut and eat the same things. Open this recipe book and pick something out that you haven't tried before and give it a go.

## 4) Invite friends over
When you cook for guests you make more effort, so invite friends and family for dinner, but make sure they invite you back!

## 5) Keep it simple
Every night doesn't have to be a gourmet banquet. Save the more complicated dishes for the weekend, plus it gives you something to look forward to.

## 6) Involve the family
This can create more mess, but it's good for children to learn from an early age about food and where it comes from, and how it's cooked.

# Breakfasts

Breakfast is the most important meal of the day – or is it?

This is such a hotly debated topic and personally I feel that the choice of food is more important than the time of day it's eaten.

Remember you are breaking a fast (Break - fast) so if you don't feel hungry, or don't class yourself as a breakfast person, you don't have to eat. The last time I checked there wasn't a law about eating breakfast, so do what feels right for your body. If you want to eat later then you can make something up to have on the run, or, at the weekend, hold off until brunch.

If you wake up hungry and love breakfast then start by avoiding commercial cereals and wheat based breakfasts like toast – even worse – toast with margarine. Choose something natural instead.

When we wake up, our blood sugar levels are usually balanced, so starting the day with protein, along with healthy fat, will help to keep them that way. It will also help you fuller for longer. If something cooked doesn't take your fancy then overnight oats or my 'meal in a glass' smoothie would be a good choice.

I understand that time can be tricky in the morning – especially if you are like me and have a school lunch box to get ready, dogs to feed and breakfast to prepare for yourself.

I tend to make things up in bulk: a large omelette that can be kept in the fridge for a few days; or I cook bacon in batches and chop it up over scrambled egg; and I make up the granola or overnight oats to have with berries.

Going continental can be a quick choice too: such as cheeses and cold meat slices or some fresh fruit.

You will find lots of lovely ideas to inspire you in this section of the book.

# Baked Porridge (V)

- SERVES **4**
- PHASE **2**

## Ingredients

150g oats

1 tsp cinnamon

1/2 tsp ground nutmeg

2 bananas, chopped

500ml milk of your choice

1 tbsp vanilla essence

100g blueberries

For when you feel like you want something carby, this dish hits the spot. It can also be served as a dessert.

This recipe contains cinnamon, which is a great spice for adding natural sweetness. Evidence suggests that it can balance sugar levels, is anti inflammatory and could also help fight bacterial and fungal infections.

## Method

1. Preheat the oven to 150°c / 300°f.

2. Mix the oats, spices and bananas together in a bowl.

3. Pour in the milk and vanilla essence, and stir until everything is combined together.

4. Pour the mixture into a Pyrex dish and top with blueberries.

5. Place on the middle shelf of the oven and bake for 35 minutes.

6. Serve warm.

## Cook's Note

• If you have a problem with dairy then you can use alternative milks such as unsweetened almond milk.

• If you are following The Harcombe Diet, low fat milk is recommended for carb meals.

# Bacon and Egg Muffins

- SERVES 4
- PHASE 2

## Ingredients

1 tbsp olive oil

4 eggs

4 bacon medallions

40g grated cheddar

Pinch cayenne pepper

My daughter calls these muffins 'Bacon cakes', which makes them great for all the family.
They are so simple to make and once cool can be wrapped in foil and used for a lunch box (no matter what your age).

## Method

1. Preheat an oven to 175°c / 350°f.

2. Oil 4 compartments of a deep muffin tray.

3. Place one piece of bacon into each of four compartments.

4. Crack each egg over the bacon.

5. Sprinkle with grated cheddar and a pinch of cayenne pepper

6. Place onto the middle shelf of an oven and bake for 20 minutes.

7. Eat warm or leave to cool and store in the fridge.

## Cook's Note

• You can leave out the cheddar cheese to make this a simple phase 1 dish.

# Baked Breakfast Omelette

- SERVES 4/6
- PHASE 2

## Ingredients

6 gluten-free sausages

2 tbsp olive oil

2 spring onions, chopped

100g cherry tomatoes, halved

100g mushrooms, sliced

250g diced pancetta or bacon lardons

8 eggs

250g full fat soft cheese

100g cheddar, grated

1 tsp dried herbs

This omelette is a one-pan wonder, which contains approximately 20g of protein per slice so it will help to keep you full for hours.

Protein is essential for repairing cells and making new ones and so is vital for the human body. We need approximately 1 gram of protein per kilogram of body weight, so that's between 50g - 80g a day for most of us (more for pregnant women and certain athletes may choose to consume more). This bacon, egg and sausage breakfast in a pan will be a healthy start to any day.

## Method

1. Preheat the oven to 175°c / 350°f.

2. Heat the oil in a large non-stick pan.

3. Fry the sausages in the pan until the skins are brown.

4. Add the spring onions, tomatoes, mushrooms, and pancetta into an oiled oven tray or large Pyrex dish.

5. Cut the sausages in half lengthways and place them as evenly as you can over the ingredients on the tray.

6. In a large bowl, whisk the eggs and soft cheese together until you have a pale yellow mixture.

7. Pour the egg mixture into the oven tray to cover the cooked ingredients then top with the cheddar and sprinkle with herbs.

8. Place on the middle shelf of the oven and bake for 35 minutes.

## Cook's Note

- Serve hot or leave to cool and store in the fridge for up to 3 days.

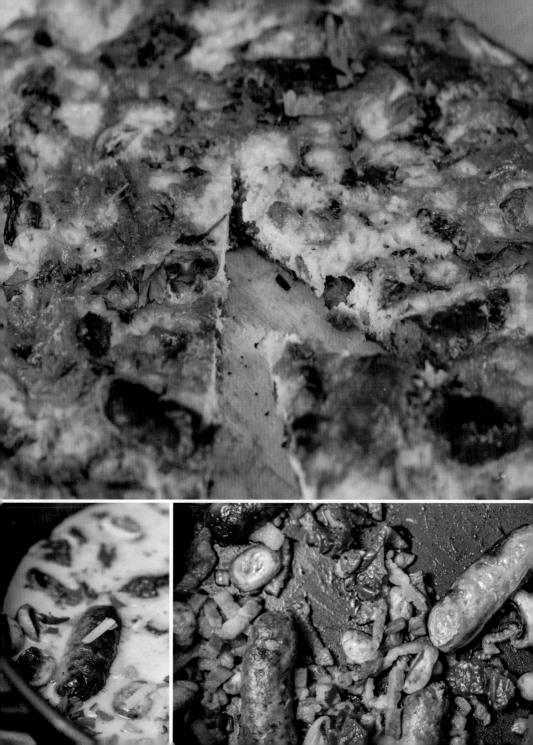

# Soda Bread (V)

- MAKES 1 LARGE LOAF
- PHASE 3

## Ingredients

300g self raising wholemeal gluten-free flour (extra for dusting)

1/2 tsp bicarbonate of soda

50g chilled butter, chopped

1 egg, beaten

25g sunflower seeds (optional)

284ml buttermilk (1 carton)

Soda bread is a traditional Irish loaf, which contains no yeast. This means that it's really quick to make, as it doesn't need to be left to rise. Baker's yeast can also cause abdominal bloating and can feed Candida, so is best kept to a minimum if you have suffered from these conditions.

Bread doesn't often feature in my daily diet, but I am often asked for a gluten-free recipe so here it is.

## Method

1. Preheat the oven to 175°c / 350°f.

2. Put the flour and the bicarbonate of soda into a mixing bowl. Then add the butter.

3. Rub the mixture between your fingers until it turns into fine crumbs.

4. Add the egg and sunflower seeds. Stir the mixture thoroughly.

5. Pour in the buttermilk and combine everything to make a thick dough.

6. Turn the dough out onto a floured bread board, or add to a large loaf tin. Sprinkle the dough with flour to prevent sticking and to make it easier to shape into a loaf. You can cut a cross into the top of the dough at this stage.

7. Place the dough onto an oven tray and bake for 30 minutes on the middle shelf of the oven.

## Cook's Note

- Leave to cool before slicing.

- Great toasted the next day and served with boiled egg.

- You can vary the recipe by adding grated cheese and spring onions, or olives and sun-dried tomatoes. Use your imagination.

# Granola (V)

- Makes approximately 10 servings
- Phase 3

Ingredients

6 tbsp coconut oil

100g unsalted butter

500g oats

2 tsp ground almonds

2 tsp vanilla essence

Commercial granola might look healthy but it often contains lots of hidden sugar. This version is much healthier.

It's handy to have some granola in the store cupboard too, for when you don't have much time. I serve mine with berries and a couple of tablespoons of natural live yoghurt.

## Method

1. Preheat the oven to 175°c / 350°f.

2. Put the coconut oil and butter into a large pan. Stir over a medium heat. Once this has melted, turn off the heat.

3. Add the oats to the pan, followed by the ground almonds and vanilla essence.

4. Spread the mixture evenly across an oven tray and bake for 15 minutes on the middle shelf of the oven.

5. Stir the granola thoroughly to make sure it's evenly cooked. You are looking to keep the oats separated, although it is nice when you find a cluster.

## Cook's Note

• Leave to cool completely before storing in an airtight container.

• It can be made in batches and keeps for around 7 days in an airtight container.

# Broccoli and Stilton Muffins (V)

- Makes 12 muffins

- Phase 2 (without the pine nuts)

## Ingredients

1 large onion, peeled and chopped

1 head of broccoli, chopped (grate the stalks)

4 tbsp olive oil (for greasing)

200g stilton cheese

10 eggs

100g pine nuts (optional)

This is a spin on a typical quiche, but without the pastry. The balance of stilton and broccoli gives a wonderful flavour to these muffins. These are ideal for vegetarians too.

It can be difficult for vegetarians to get enough complete protein into their diet, so regularly including eggs and cheese, along with pulses, nuts and seeds will help.

## Method

1. Preheat the oven to 175°c / 350°f.

2. Oil the muffin tin with some olive oil and place in the oven to warm up.

3. Add the onion and broccoli to a large mixing bowl.

4. Crumble the cheese in to the onion and broccoli bowl and mix thoroughly.

5. In a separate bowl, whisk together the eggs. Then combine all of the ingredients.

6. Remove the muffin tin from the oven and add two tablespoons of the mixture to each segment. If there is any mixture remaining, top up the muffins equally and sprinkle with pine nuts.

7. Place in the oven for 20 minutes.

## Cook's Note

• Serve warm or leave to cool and store in the fridge for up to 3 days.

• Always save the broccoli stalks for soups or stir fry dishes, or grate them into a salad; they contain lots of calcium.

# Super Smoothie (V)

- SERVES 2

- PHASE 3

## Ingredients

1 small ripe banana, chopped

1 tbsp sunflower seeds

Handful of kale

100g frozen berries

300ml almond milk

1/2 tsp vanilla essence

This recipe gives you a meal in a glass and is a rich source of a couple of vital nutrients: Sunflower seeds are unbeatable for vitamin E and the kale gives you a good dose of vitamin C.

## Method

1. Add the banana, seeds, kale, berries and milk with the vanilla essence into the blender.

2. Blend on the highest setting for 1 minute until the mixture is smooth. Serve immediately.

## Cook's Note

• You will need a blender for this recipe.

• As this recipe serves two, you can freeze the leftovers or cover and keep in the fridge for the next day. Just make sure to stir thoroughly before drinking it.

• You can make this Harcombe Phase 2 friendly by leaving out the sunflower seeds. Almond milk is practically water nowadays!

# Overnight Oats (V)

- SERVES 1
- PHASE 2

## Ingredients

50g oats

1/2 tsp cinnamon

150g fat free Natural Live Yoghurt

50g blueberries

1 apple, peeled, cored and grated

This recipe can help when you don't have much time in the morning. Make sure you use a 'live' or 'bio' yoghurt as it will contain good bacteria to help keep your gut happy.

## Method

1. Mix the oats and cinnamon together in a large mixing bowl, using a large metal spoon.

2. Pour the yoghurt, blueberries, and apple into the mixture and stir together.

3. Place the mixture into a jar or glass and cover with foil. Keep the mixture in the fridge overnight. Breakfast is served.

## Cook's Note

- Try using other fruits to add your personal touch.

# Tapas

Tapas dishes are great for informal entertaining. These recipes are bursting with flavour and if you find a favourite, it can be served as a bigger portion for a main meal.

# Garlic Dough Balls (V)

## Ingredients

180g ground almonds

100g Parmesan cheese, grated

2 eggs, beaten

250g mozzarella cheese

1 tsp pesto

1/2 tsp garlic powder for the recipe and a bit extra for serving

3 tbsp butter, melted

This dough ball recipe is so more'ish. This was proven when we did the photo shoot for this recipe book and the cameraman ate them all!
Garlic is one of my favourite flavours, it's a wonder food as it is anti-fungal, anti-viral and anti-bacterial. If you feel like you have a cold coming then ramp up the garlic.

## Method

1. Preheat the oven to 175°c / 350°f.

2. Add the ground almonds, Parmesan and eggs to a large mixing bowl and stir thoroughly.

3. Shred the mozzarella cheese and mix this in with the other ingredients.

4. Add the pesto and garlic powder.

5. Take a small handful of the dough and shape into 14 balls, roughly the size of golf balls.

6. Place each one on greaseproof paper on an oven tray.

7. Roast for 15 minutes.

8. Spoon the butter over the roasted balls and sprinkle with garlic powder. Serve hot.

## Cook's note

• Replace the dry garlic for fresh if you want an extra kick.

# Roasted Nuts (V)

- SERVES 4
(IF YOU ARE WILLING TO SHARE)
- PHASE 3

## Ingredients

100g cashews
100g almonds
50g sunflower seeds
50g sesame seeds
1 tbsp olive oil
1/2 tsp salt
1 tsp chilli powder

If you love savoury snacks, then you will love these crunchy nuts. They can be eaten alone, or sprinkled over a salad.

## Method

1. Preheat the oven to 175°c / 350°f.

2. Add all of the nuts and seeds to a large mixing bowl and then pour in the olive oil, salt and chilli powder.

3. Mix all the ingredients with a wooden spoon and spread them evenly across an oven tray.

4. Place the tray into the oven on the highest shelf and roast for 20 minutes.

5. Remove the tray from the oven and use some kitchen towel to wipe off any excess oil.

6. Leave to cool then serve.

## Cook's Note

- Store any leftovers in an airtight container.

# Prawn and Salmon Roulade

- SERVES 4
- PHASE 2

### Ingredients

250g full fat soft cheese

10 sprigs of chives, finely chopped

1 lemon (for the juice)

250g smoked salmon

1 cucumber, sliced

250g cooked king prawns

Smoked salmon and cream cheese is such a great combination. This recipe is so fresh and full of flavour. There is no cooking involved, so it is really quick and easy to prepare.

## Method

1. Put the soft cheese and chives in a mixing bowl.

2. Squeeze the lemon juice into the mixing bowl, making sure that no lemon pips fall into the mixture. Then mix thoroughly with a large metal spoon.

3. Take a piece of smoked salmon and lay it flat on a baking tray. Spread a tablespoon of the mixture over the salmon and roll up to make your roulade. Then slice the roulade into 1cm wide rolls.

## Cook's Note

- For tapas, thread a slice of cucumber onto a cocktail stick, then sit the salmon on top and finish with a king prawn.

- Keep in the fridge until ready to serve.

# Stuffed Goats Cheese Peppers (V)

- SERVES 4
- PHASE 2

## Ingredients

2 red peppers

2 handfuls of spinach

200g goat's cheese, sliced

1/2 tsp ground nutmeg

This is a perfect vegetarian meal, or it can be used as a side dish to accompany chicken or fish. You can also simply enjoy it alone with a salad.

## Method

1. Preheat the oven to 175°c / 350°f.

2. Cut the pepper in half lengthways and scoop out the seeds, then wash them. Try to keep the stalk intact if possible to help retain the pepper's shape.

3. Place the peppers onto an oiled baking tray and stuff each pepper with uncooked spinach.

4. Push equal amounts of the goats cheese into each pepper half.

5. Sprinkle the peppers with nutmeg and then place in the oven for 30 minutes.

# Garlic Baked Camembert (V)

## Ingredients

3 garlic cloves,
peeled and halved

Handful of fresh
thyme or rosemary

1 whole camembert
cheese (in wooden box)

This is what weekend treats are all about: rich creamy and roast garlic to use as a mini fondue all to yourself. You can of course share as part of a tapas table too.

## Method

1. Preheat the oven to 175°c / 350°f.

2. Push the garlic cloves into the camembert cheese, until you can no longer see them.

3. Next, push the thyme or rosemary into the camembert cheese. The sprigs should stick out of the top.

4. Bake for 20 minutes.

## Cook's Note

- When you cut this, the cheese will melt out – serve immediately.
- This makes a lovely dip or sauce for meat or fish.

# Super Sardine Pâté

## Ingredients

125g unsalted butter, melted

4 x 200g tins of sardines in brine, drained

1 lemon, halved

1 tbsp Italian herbs

Until I made this recipe, I didn't think I liked sardines. It was the thought of crunching through the tiny little bones that put me off, but this method gives you a super smooth pâté that tastes similar to tuna. The tiny bones are the most nutritious part of sardines, so they are important to consume. The bones are especially high in calcium and vitamin D. If you avoid dairy, sardines are an ideal way of getting your bone nutrients.

## Method

1. Add the sardines and butter to the food processor.

2. Squeeze all of the lemon juice into the food processor, making sure no lemon pips fall into the mixture.

3. Sprinkle the herbs into the food processor and blend for a few minutes, until you get a smooth paste.

4. Turn out the pâté into an airtight container or ramekin.

## Cook's Note

- This can be eaten instantly as a dip or set in the fridge for a few hours for pâté.

- It will stay fresh in the fridge for 3 days or 3 months in the freezer.

# Smoked Mackerel Pâté

- Serves 2
- Phase 2

## Ingredients

125g smoked mackerel fillets, skinned

50g full fat cream cheese

1 lemon, halved

I do love pâtés, I often make them for lunch and use celery as crudités to scoop up.

This is a recipe that's so easy to make, as there is no cooking involved. It also freezes well so you can make it in batches.

## Method

1. Add the smoked mackerel and cream cheese to the food processor.

2. Squeeze the lemon juice into the food processor, ensuring no lemon pips fall in.

3. Blend the mixture together.

4. Once the mixture has blended, transfer to an airtight container and store in the fridge.

# Lentil Pâté (V)

- Serves 4
- Phase 2

## Ingredients

2 tbsp olive oil

1 onion, peeled and finely diced

200g lentils

150ml boiling water

50g tomato purée

4 tbsp white wine

2 tsp dried herbs

Lentils have such an earthy wholesome taste and make a nice thick pâté. Lentils are also a bit of a 'superfood' in the vegetarian world. They are a useful provider of the B vitamins and especially good for minerals: copper; iron; magnesium; manganese; phosphorus; potassium; selenium and zinc.

## Method

1. Heat the olive oil in a large pan.

2. Add the onion to the pan and fry it for a few minutes, until soft.

3. Add the lentils and pour over the boiling water. Allow to simmer on low for around 20 minutes, until the water has been absorbed.

4. Stir in the tomato purée, wine, and herbs.

5. Either add to a blender or mash with a fork.

6. Transfer the pâté to an airtight container and leave to cool before leaving to set in the fridge.

## Cook's note

• The wine would strictly make this a Phase 3 dish, but the wine will be simmered off so don't worry about this small cheat.

# Pancetta and Chorizo in Red Wine

## Ingredients

1 tbsp olive oil

100g pancetta, diced

200g chorizo, sliced

3 shallots, peeled and finely chopped

4 garlic cloves, finely chopped

2 tbsp tomato purée

2 tbsp smoked paprika

100g black olives (make sure they are pitted)

200ml dry red wine

Pinch of salt

Pinch of pepper

This is one of my favourite meals. The red wine gives it a really rich flavour. I usually enjoy it with a green salad.

## Method

1. Heat the olive oil in a frying pan.

2. Add the pancetta and cook for a few minutes, until crispy.

3. Add the chorizo to the pan to fry for a few minutes. The red spices should start to colour the pan.

4. Add the shallots and garlic to the pan. Then leave to sauté for a few minutes.

5. Squeeze in the tomato purée and add the smoked paprika, olives and red wine. Simmer for 20 minutes until the wine evaporates and leaves you with a thicker sauce.

6. Season with salt and pepper. Serve hot.

## Cook's Note

• The wine would strictly make this a Phase 3 dish, but the wine will be simmered off so don't worry about this small cheat.

# Roasted Chickpeas (V)

- SERVES 4
- PHASE 2

## Ingredients

800g chickpeas, drained

6 tbsp tamari (gluten-free soy sauce)

Chickpeas are full of fibre and nutrients and are especially valuable for vegetarians. These can be eaten alone as a snack or mixed into a salad.

## Method

1. Preheat the oven to 175°c / 350°f.

2. Tip the chickpeas onto an oven tray and cover with the tamari.

3. Place in the oven on the highest shelf and bake for 15 minutes.

4. Remove the tray from the oven to give them another stir. Place back in the oven and bake for a further 15 minutes.

5. Leave to cool before serving.

## Cook's Note

• You can get gluten-free Tamari sauce without sugar – check the gluten-free part of the supermarket and/or the oriental section. The only ingredients necessary are water, soybeans and salt. If there's anything else that's natural, it's OK. Anything you don't recognise – keep looking for another brand.

# Parmesan Chicken Bites

## Ingredients

500g chicken breast, diced

2 eggs

200g Parmesan cheese, grated

Black pepper

My daughter loves these and thinks they are chicken nuggets, and in a way they are! They are great for all the family and work well with turkey and salmon too.

## Method

1. Preheat the oven to 175°c / 350°f.

2. Whisk the eggs together in a bowl and sprinkle the grated Parmesan onto a plate.

3. Using a fork, dip the chicken pieces into the egg mixture, followed by the Parmesan, then place onto a baking tray.

4. Continue the process until all the chicken is covered. Then season with plenty of pepper.

5. Place in the oven and bake for 30 minutes.

## Cook's Note

• For a quicker option you can place the chicken pieces into a plastic bag then pour in some of the egg mixture, then the Parmesan, and shake.

# Pea, Mint and Feta Salad (V)

## Ingredients

1 (100g) bag of
rocket leaves

1 sweet romaine
lettuce

250ml boiling water

100g frozen peas

1 lemon, halved

2 sprigs of mint leaves,
chopped

2 tbsp olive oil

100g feta cheese,
cubed

These flavours are so fresh and make a perfect summer salad together.

Mint is a great digestive aid: you can use any spare leaves to make up a tea with boiling water and a slice of lemon.

## Method

1. Wash and drain the rocket and sweet romaine. Roughly chop the leaves as desired (the rocket may need little chopping, the romaine will need more).

2. Pour the boiling water over the peas and leave them to thaw while you make the dressing.

3. In a mixing bowl, squeeze in the lemon juice, making sure no lemon pips fall in. Add the olive oil and mint leaves and mix thoroughly.

4. Drain the peas and mix the leaves together in a bowl. Pour over the dressing and top with the feta cheese.

## Cook's Note

• You can add some grilled chicken or flaked salmon to make this into a main course.

# Spicy Belly Pork

- SERVES 4
- PHASE 2

## Ingredients

3 tbsp smoked paprika

3 tbsp mild chilli powder

3 tbsp balsamic vinegar

3 tbsp olive oil

500g belly pork, cubed (outdoor bred if you can source well)

This is where being able to eat fat and lose weight is at its tastiest. Belly pork is great value and takes on flavour well. This works well on the barbeque too.

## Method

1. Preheat the oven to 190°c / 375°f.

2. In a bowl, combine the spices with the vinegar and oil, then add the pork and stir until you have an even coating.

3. Place onto an oven tray and bake for 35 minutes.

## Cook's Note

• You can place these on cocktail sticks if you are serving tapas.

• If you leave out the vinegar, this can be fine for Phase 1 too.

# Hot and Spicy Prawns

## Ingredients

2 tbsp olive oil

2 chillies, deseeded
and chopped

2 cloves of garlic,
finely sliced

16 large prawns

1 lemon, halved

## Method

1. Heat the olive oil in a frying pan.

2. When the oil is hot, add the chillies and garlic
and fry for 1 minute.

3. Add the prawns and fry for a further 4-5 minutes,
turning regularly.

4. Transfer the prawns to a warmed dish and pour
the oil from the frying pan over the prawns.

5. Squeeze the lemon juice over the prawns,
making sure no pips fall in.

6. Serve immediately.

# Beef and Horseradish with Tomato

- SERVES 4
- PHASE 2

### Ingredients

6 tbsp horseradish

6 slices of cold beef

18 cherry tomatoes, halved

Cocktail sticks

A simple but tasty meaty tapas dish.

## Method

1. Take a tablespoon of horseradish and spread it over the beef slice, then roll it up.

2. Cut the beef into 1cm pieces and thread onto a cocktail stick.

3. Top and tail the cocktail stick with a cherry tomato.

## Cook's Note

• You can get Horseradish sauces without sugar and other nasties. Horseradish (of course), vinegar, oil and seasoning are likely ingredients. Mustard and egg yolk are also possible. You don't need sugar or flour or anything you don't recognise. You can always make your own with 100g of peeled and minced horseradish root, 50ml white wine vinegar and salt and pepper to taste.

• Keep in the fridge until ready to serve.

# Chorizo, Halloumi and Blueberry Kebabs

- SERVES 4

- PHASE 3

## Ingredients

200g dried chorizo sausage, sliced

100g halloumi, sliced

100g blueberries

4 kebab sticks

Halloumi is a cooking cheese: once it has been under the grill or barbeque you get a crispy outside and a chewy cheesy middle. It's quite salty, so the blueberries help to balance this out and the chorizo gives a kick of spice.

## Method

1. Preheat the oven to 200°c / 400°f.

2. Thread the chorizo onto the kebab sticks alternately with halloumi and blueberries.

3. Grill each side of the kebab for 4 minutes.

## Cook's Note

• Serve with a green salad, or eat them straight off the stick.

# Soups

When people hear that I follow a gluten-free diet they ask: "what do you eat instead of sandwiches for lunch?" – and the answer is often soup or salad.

I always like to make soup with the option of turning it into a sauce, so that I have a supply of freshly made sauces in the freezer. For example, the tomato soup recipe can be used as a Bolognese sauce, or add chilli and use for a chilli beef pie recipe.

The butternut squash soup can be used as a curry sauce by adding chicken and a bag of spinach.

If you like spicy food, then turn your favourite curry sauce into a soup.

Soup is really filling, and if it's blended it's easy to digest. Granny wasn't mad when she said "chicken soup will make you better"!

# Spiced Butternut Squash and Coconut (can be V)

- SERVES **4**
- PHASE **3**

## Ingredients

800g butternut squash, peeled, deseeded and cubed

4 tbsp olive oil

3 chillies, whole

1 tsp garam masala

1 tsp ground cumin

6 garlic cloves

1 onion, peeled and finely chopped

600ml chicken or vegetable stock

200ml coconut milk

1 lime

Salt and black pepper for seasoning

Coconut milk makes this soup so rich and creamy without the need for dairy products. This can be used as a curry sauce too. Just add meat or fish of your choice with extra vegetables.

## Method

1. Preheat the oven to 200°c / 400°f.

2. Drizzle the butternut squash with half the olive oil. Toss with the chillies and spices.

3. Roast for 20 minutes. Scatter over the garlic and roast for a further 30 minutes.

4. Heat the remaining olive oil in a pan. Add the onion to the pan and allow to soften.

5. When the butternut squash is tender, discard 2 of the chillies.

6. Put the spiced butternut squash into a blender or food processor, with the remaining chilli, onion and 200ml stock. Blend everything until smooth.

7. Return the liquid mixture to the pan and add the coconut milk and the remaining stock.

8. Simmer for 20 minutes. Halve the lime and squeeze in the juice, making sure that no lime pips fall into the pan. Season well and serve hot.

## Cook's Note

- Vegetable stock adds another valuable vegetarian recipe to your repertoire. Chick peas could be added to make a main meal curry, or just enjoy the soup.

- We've marked this as Phase 3 for The Harcombe Diet because it is strictly a mix meal. Per portion, 200g of butternut squash contains approximately 24g of carbohydrate and no fat; 50ml of coconut milk contains approximately 12g of fat and 3g of carbohydrate. However, this could be used as the base for a Phase 2 fat or carb meal – especially if something is added to make the sauce go further (and therefore each portion of sauce becomes smaller). Chicken would go really well, for example. Plus – when you are doing well in Phase 2, a little flex like this is really not going to spoil progress. Sticking to real food is the single best thing that you can do.

# Mean Green Soup – Spinach, Celeriac and Courgette (V)

- SERVES 4
- PHASE 1

## Ingredients

2 tbsp of olive oil

1 onion, peeled and finely chopped

1 celeriac, peeled and cubed

3 small courgettes, peeled and chopped into small pieces

600ml boiling water

2 tbsp vegetable bouillon

1 (100g) bag of spinach

Celeriac makes a great alternative to potatoes without the high carb intake and it gives this soup a lovely thick texture.

## Method

1. Heat the oil in a large pan.

2. Fry the onion in the olive oil for a few minutes, until it starts to soften.

3. Add the celeriac and courgettes to the pan.

4. Add the water and bouillon powder to the pan then leave to simmer for 20 minutes, or until the vegetables are soft.

5. Add the bag of spinach and place the lid on the pan. The spinach will wilt in a few minutes.

6. Remove from the heat and blend everything in a blender or food processor.

7. Reheat gently to serve.

## Cook's Note

• Add a swirl of double cream for a Phase 2, creamier soup.

# Beetroot Soup (can be V)

- SERVES 4
- PHASE 1

## Ingredients

2 tbsp olive oil

1 onion, peeled and finely chopped

3 large fresh beetroot, peeled and cubed

10 cherry tomatoes, halved

2 beef (or vegetable) stock cubes

350ml of water

2 garlic cloves

Beetroot has a natural sweet, earthy taste and is full of fibre. Beware of having purple palms after chopping up the beetroot!

## Method

1. Heat the olive oil in a large saucepan.

2. Add the onion to the pan and cook for a few minutes, until it looks translucent.

3. Add the beetroot to the pan and leave it to sweat for 5 minutes on a low heat. Then add the cherry tomatoes.

4. Add the stock cubes, water, and garlic and bring to the boil. Leave to simmer for 30 minutes.

5. Liquidise using a stick blender then reheat gently to serve hot.

## Cook's Note

• Beef stock complements the beetroot flavour really well, but this is another recipe where vegetable stock can be used instead for a vegetarian recipe.

# Spiced Parsnip and Apple (can be V)

- SERVES 4
- PHASE 2

## Ingredients

20g butter

1 tbsp olive oil

2 onions, peeled and diced

2 garlic cloves, chopped

3 tbsp curry powder

700g parsnips, peeled and diced

2 pints vegetable/chicken stock

Pinch of salt

Pinch of pepper

175g cooking apples, peeled, cored and diced

If you have parsnips left over (maybe after Thanksgiving or Christmas? Or just in the seasonal organic delivery veg box), then this is a great way to use them up.

## Method

1. Heat the butter and olive oil in a large sauce pan, until the butter starts to foam.

2. Add the onions and soften for about 5 minutes before adding the garlic. Leave to cook for a further 2 minutes.

3. Mix together with the curry powder and stir.

4. Add the parsnips to the pan along with the apples.

5. Stir well and pour in the stock, and add some seasoning.

6. Leave to simmer gently for half an hour without a lid.

7. Remove from the heat and blend everything in a blender or food processor.

8. Place back onto the heat and warm through. Serve hot.

## Cook's note

- Opt for vegetable stock for another great vegetarian option.

# Roast Pepper and Sun-dried Tomato (V)

- SERVES 4
- PHASE 1

## Ingredients

500g salad tomatoes

4 garlic cloves

1 onion, halved

3 red peppers, halved and deseeded

2 tbsp olive oil

25g butter

2 celery sticks, finely chopped

450ml vegetable stock

2 tbsp tomato purée

1 tbsp sun-dried tomato paste

1 tsp chilli flakes

Pinch of salt

Pinch of pepper

I always save a portion of this soup for my freezer so I have a quick Bolognese sauce at the ready.

## Method

1. Preheat the oven to 200°c / 400°f.

2. Place the tomatoes, garlic, onion and pepper halves (cut side down) onto a baking tray and drizzle with olive oil.

3. Bake on the top shelf of the oven for 30 minutes, until roasted.

4. Melt the butter over a medium heat and sauté the celery for 4-5 minutes.

5. Add the vegetable stock, tomato purée, sun-dried tomato paste and chilli flakes together and mix well.

6. Remove from the heat and leave to one side.

7. When the vegetables are roasted, remove the peel from the garlic and onion, and roughly chop them. Add to the pan along with the tomatoes.

8. Place back on a low to medium heat for 20 minutes.

9. Blend with a hand blender, until smooth.

10. Season well and gently simmer, until the soup is at a suitable temperature to eat.

# Mains

I often get a text message from my husband, "What's for tea?" So now I say, "Look at the planner!"

To make things simple, every few months I like to make a planner for our meals. '7 dinners for 7 days'. We vote as a family for our favourites and make sure there is always a mix of chicken, red meat (because it's far more nutritious than white meat), some fish and a creamy dish. Then I make a shopping list and we have these dishes for a while until we fancy a change. It's much easier to live like this instead of getting home, opening the fridge and wondering what's for tea. You also save money, as you only buy what you need.

Of course, if you have guests or fancy something different on the weekend, then you can – It's your tummy! So fill it full of lovely (real) food.

# Oven Roasted Ratatouille (V)

- SERVES **4**
- PHASE **1**

## Ingredients

2 large onions, peeled and diced

2 aubergines, diced

2 peppers, deseeded and diced (red or yellow)

2 courgettes, sliced

6 cloves garlic, peeled and chopped

1 tbsp olive oil

1 tbsp smoked paprika

Pinch of salt

1/2 tbsp mixed herbs

1kg passata

Ratatouille is a great staple meal. The recipe uses lower starchy vegetables and passata so it can be used with either carb, or fat meals. Passata is a thick tomato sauce made from sieved tomatoes. It comes without the added sugar and nasties of commercial sauces and is readily available in super markets. I like to make this in bulk and freeze it in portions.

## Method

1. Preheat the oven to 175°C/ 350°F.

2. Place the vegetables onto a large baking tray or two smaller ones (you want one layer).

3. Drizzle over some olive oil and sprinkle over the spices, salt and herbs.

4. Roast for 15 minutes and stir through. Roast for a further 20 minutes.

5. Once cooked, remove the tray and pour over the passata.

6. Stir through and serve.

## Cook's Note

• Feel free to spice this up with chilli powder, or any other flavour you'd like to add.

• For a fat meal, try using it as a sauce with meat balls and cheese, or as a side for a salmon fillet or chicken.

• For a carb meal serve with brown rice, quinoa, jacket potato or sweet potato wedges.

# Pea, Mint and Feta Frittata (V)

- SERVES 4
- PHASE 2

## Ingredients

2 tbsp olive oil

1 large onion, peeled and finely diced

200ml boiled water

200g frozen peas

1 courgette, peeled and grated

6 eggs

100ml double cream

8 fresh mint leaves, finely chopped

100g feta cheese, cubed

100g cheddar, grated

Frittata or crustless quiche can work with so many fillings, but this one is a little bit special and it is great for vegetarians.

## Method

1. Preheat the grill to 175°C / 350°F.

2. Heat the olive oil in a pan.

3. Add the onion to the pan and leave to sauté on a low heat.

4. Pour the boiled water over the peas in a large bowl and leave to one side to defrost.

5. Add the courgette to the onion and stir well.

6. Drain the peas and add these to the pan.

7. Put the eggs and cream in a mixing bowl, and whisk until you have a thick, pale yellow mixture. Then stir in the mint.

8. Pour the egg mixture into the frying pan and turn up the heat to help seal the egg. Then mix both mixtures together.

9. Spread the feta and cheddar over the frittata.

10. Turn down the heat to the lowest setting and cook for 5 minutes.

11. Place under the grill to brown off for a further 3 minutes.

## Cook's Note

- Serve warm or cold, for breakfast, lunch or tea.

# Slow Cooked Beef and Aubergine Curry

- Serves 6
- Phase 1

## Ingredients

2 tbsp olive oil

750g braising beef, diced

1 onion, peeled and finely diced

2 large garlic cloves, finely diced

4 tbsp of garam masala

2 tbsp smoked paprika

1 tbsp chilli powder

800g tomatoes, chopped (two 400g tins will work well)

100g tomato purée

150ml water

4 large aubergines, diced

Salt and pepper

(100g grated cream of coconut)

Handful of coriander, finely chopped

As a nutritionist, knowing the nutritional content of red meat, it always amazes me that it gets such a bad press. Red meat is far more nutritious than white meat – and tastier. It is full of B vitamins – our mind, mood and muscle vitamins – and of course rich in iron and zinc. Ideally try to source beef from pasture living cattle – this is important for your health, the animal's health and the health of the planet (cows rejuvenate soil in a natural circle of life with the grass and micro flora that they swallow, host and regurgitate).

## Method

1. Preheat the oven to 175°C / 350°F.

2. Heat the oil in a large non-stick pan and add the beef. Keep stirring to seal each side.

3. Add the onion and garlic to the pan. Turn the heat down to the lowest setting.

4. Add the spices to the beef and pour over the tomatoes, tomato puree and water. Leave to simmer.

5. Place the aubergine onto two baking trays and sprinkle with olive oil. Season with salt and pepper.

6. Place in the oven for 30 minutes.

7. When the aubergine is cooked, add it to the curry and stir through.

8. Simmer on low for 3 hours.

9. When you are ready to serve, add the grated creamed coconut and coriander.

## Cook's Note

- Serve warm or cold, for breakfast, lunch or tea.

- Serve hot with our non bread (see side dishes for the recipe)

- Strict Phase 1 would leave out the coconut cream, but each portion ends up with approximately 15g so you may choose not to worry about this for the benefit of the richness of the flavour. The famous Harcombe Diet butternut squash curry uses coconut cream with the same caveat – probably worth the flex for the flavour benefit, but leave out if you're an all or nothing type.

# Beef Bourguignon

## Ingredients

2 tbsp olive oil

200g bacon

1kg braising beef, diced

3 shallots, peeled and finely diced

2 tbsp corn flour

1 large carrot, finely chopped

1 stick celery, finely chopped

200g button mushrooms, halved

500ml red wine (I use a Merlot)

200ml water

3 beef stock cubes

Handful of thyme, chopped

This recipe includes a decent dose of red wine, which goes really well with the beef in terms of flavour and it's not a bad 'digestif' too! I always serve this on Boxing Day, because it's great to make ahead for a crowd and to leave to simmer. A rich classic, which I like to serve with mashed celeriac and green vegetables.

## Method

1. Heat the oil in a large non-stick pan.

2. Fry the bacon until brown and crispy.

3. Put the beef in the pan and then fry it until it is sealed on all sides.

4. Stir the shallots into the pan and sprinkle the corn flour into the pan – coating the pieces of beef.

5. Add the carrot, celery and mushrooms to the pan.

6. Pour in the wine and water, and cook on a low heat for 3 hours.

7. When you are ready to serve, crumble in the stock cubes and thyme, then turn up the heat to thicken the sauce.

8. Serve hot.

## Cook's Note

• Don't worry about the tiny amount of corn flour. There will be so little in each portion as not to worry about and it is important for thickening. Don't worry unduly about the red wine either – much of it burns off in cooking.

# Luxurious Low Carb Fish Pie

- SERVES 6
- PHASE 2

## Ingredients

500g (1 large) celeriac, peeled and cubed

500ml boiling water

Salt and pepper

50g butter

25g corn flour

250ml whole milk

100g strong cheddar, grated

2 salmon fillets, diced

250g cod steaks (or other white fish), diced

250g smoked haddock, diced

200g prawns

100g frozen peas

1 tsp fresh or dried parsley

## Method

1. Preheat the oven to 175°C / 350°F.

2. Put the celeriac in a large saucepan.

3. Pour boiling water over the celeriac and add 1/2 a teaspoon of salt. Bring everything to the boil and leave to simmer for 15 minutes until the celeriac is soft.

4. While the celeriac cooks, make your roux sauce by melting the butter in a large non-stick pan.

5. Using a wooden spoon, stir in the corn flour until it combines to make a smooth paste. Season with salt and pepper.

6. Pour in the milk and stir through until you have a thick white sauce. Add 50g of the grated cheese to the mix.

7. Add the fish to the white sauce with the peas and leave to cook through for 10 minutes. Then transfer to a Pyrex dish.

8. The celeriac should be ready for mashing. Work quickly to mash it, then cover the fish evenly. Sprinkle with the remaining cheese.

9. Place on the middle shelf in the oven and bake for 30 minutes. Serve hot with the (fresh) parsley sprinkled on top.

## Cook's Note

• Don't worry about the tiny amount of corn flour. There will be so little in each portion as not to worry about and it is important for thickening.

• We didn't suggest an alternative milk for this one, as the cheese makes it unsuitable for those who can't tolerate dairy – sorry!

Oily fish, such as salmon, is rich in essential omega-3 oils. Essential in nutrition means something that we must consume in our diet, because the body can't make it. The essential fats (omega-3 and omega-6) are called essential for this reason: we can't make them, so we must eat them.

This low carb fish pie has been a true family favourite in our house, since my daughter was a baby. It is a great way to introduce fish to children and even grownups who aren't fish fans. They will be after this.

# Slow Roast Chinese Duck with Egg Pancake Rolls

- SERVES 4
- PHASE 2

## Ingredients

4 duck breasts

4 tsp salt

3 tbsp gluten-free soy sauce (tamari)

3tbsp balsamic vinegar

3 tbsp of water

1 tbsp five spice

3 cloves of garlic, chopped

1 inch piece of ginger, peeled and grated

200g blackberries

## For the pancakes

1 tbsp olive oil

3 eggs

Pinch of baking power

1 carrot, grated

Bunch of fresh coriander, chopped

## Method

### For the Duck

1. Preheat the oven to 150°C / 300°F.

2. Heat a heavy based frying pan without any oil, until smoking hot.

3. Score the skin of the duck breasts and rub with a tsp of salt.

4. Place the duck breasts skin side down and fry for 5 minutes.

5. Place the duck breasts in an oven dish.

6. In a bowl, mix together the soy sauce, balsamic vinegar and water. Add the five spice, garlic and ginger, then pour over the duck.

7. Place the blackberries around the duck breasts.

8. Place on a middle shelf in the oven for 3 hours.

9. Remove from the oven and leave to cool for 15 minutes.

10. Shred the duck and sieve through any remaining sauce and leave to one side.

### For the pancakes

1. Heat the oil in a small frying pan.

2. Whisk the eggs with the baking powder.

3. For 4 pancakes pour in one quarter of the mixture and fry like a pancake.

4. Repeat the process until you have 4 pancakes.

5. Fill the pancake with duck, carrot and coriander salad and drizzle any remaining juices from the pan. Then roll up to serve.

Duck is a quite a fatty meat, so this is a hearty fat meal with *The Harcombe Diet*. This dish sends a lovely aroma around the house while cooking and if you are missing Chinese food then it's certainly worth the effort.

# St. David's Day Cawl

- SERVES 6
- PHASE 2 (CAN BE ADAPTED TO PHASE 1)

## Ingredients

2 tbsp olive oil

600g lamb, boned shoulder, diced

2 onions, peeled and roughly chopped

2 celery sticks, sliced

2 carrots, peeled and sliced

600ml lamb or vegetable stock

2 parsnips, peeled and chopped

1 small swede, peeled and chopped

2 leeks, trimmed and sliced

1 large celeriac, peeled and chopped

250ml red wine

Dash of Worcester sauce

2 tsp dried thyme

Salt and pepper to taste

I'm proud to be Welsh and it's traditional to serve this recipe on St David's day but it can be eaten at anytime of the year.

Soups and stews have been shown to keep people fuller for longer due to the water content. Get yourself a soup flask and take some to work for lunch – beats sandwiches any day!

## Method

1. Heat the oil in a large pan.

2. Stir the lamb in with the oil for a few minutes until the meat is brown.

3. Add the onions, celery and carrots and then turn the heat down to the lowest setting and place the lid on the pan to let the vegetables sweat through.

4. Pour in the stock and leave to simmer on low for 2 hours.

5. Add the parsnips, swede, leeks and celeriac to the pan.

6. Pour in the wine, Worcester sauce, and thyme and leave to cook on a medium heat for a further 35 minutes until the vegetables are softened.

7. Season well and serve.

## Cook's Note

• If there is any liquid left over you can keep it as a stock for gravy.

• You can leave out the red wine and Worcester sauce to make this a Phase 1 dish. The dash of Worcester sauce will be fine to leave in – even in Phase 1 – to be honest.

# Slow Cooked Beef Ragu

- SERVES 8
- PHASE 2 (LEAVE OUT CORN FLOUR AND WINE FOR A PHASE 1 VARIANT)

## Ingredients

2 tbsp olive oil

250g smoked pancetta/ bacon, finely diced

1kg braising beef, diced

1 large onion, peeled and finely chopped

2 cloves garlic, peeled and chopped

2 sticks celery, finely chopped

8 salad tomatoes, quartered

2 carrots, peeled and grated

2 x 500g cartons of passata

6 tbsp tomato puree

1 glass dry white wine

1 tsp dried Italian herbs

2 tsp corn flour (optional)

This is a traditional Bolognese sauce with a twist, using chunky pieces of beef and pancetta/bacon, which is slow cooked for several hours in a rich tomato and herb sauce.

This dish is a perfect 'bulk cooking' recipe. When making a slow cooked dish I tend to make it in bulk and freeze anything left over.

## Method

1. Heat the olive oil in a large pan, then add the pancetta/bacon and cook on a high heat for 5 minutes. This helps to get a really nice base flavour for the ragu.

2. Add the beef and cook for 5 minutes, stirring continuously to make sure each piece is sealed.

3. Add the onion, garlic, celery, quartered tomatoes and carrots and sauté with the meat for 5 minutes.

4. Add the passata, tomato puree and wine along with the herbs.

5. Bring everything to the boil and then turn the heat down to the lowest setting and leave the dish to simmer for 3 hours without a lid. The sauce will thicken during the cooking process. If you would like a thicker sauce, add a couple of teaspoons of corn flour to a cup half filled with cold water to make a paste. Use a fork to mix through any lumps and then stir this into your sauce.

## Cook's Note

- I like to serve this with salad and garlic dough balls.

- The best part about getting to know your local butcher is that s/he will prepare meat for you. I always ask mine to dice up my meat, which saves so much time in the kitchen.

# Breton Chicken

- SERVES 4
- PHASE 2

## Ingredients

2 tbsp olive oil

1 large onion, peeled and diced

4 garlic cloves, chopped

4 chicken breasts, cubed

1 gammon steak, cubed (or bacon)

2 tbsp corn flour or arrowroot powder

300ml double cream

200g cheddar cheese, grated

300ml water

1 large broccoli, chopped into small florets

1 large leek, sliced

Here is why I don't often eat carbs – because I can eat things like this without gaining weight. Smoked bacon with chicken in a creamy sauce – what's not to like?

## Method

1. Heat the oil in a large non-stick pan.

2. Add the onion and garlic to the pan and sauté for 5 minutes, on a low heat.

3. Add the chicken breasts and gammon. Stir until all of the meat is sealed.

4. Sprinkle over the corn flour, making sure that you coat all of the meat.

5. Pour in the cream, grated cheese and water.

6. Add the broccoli and leeks to the pan and leave to simmer on the lowest heat for 30 minutes – until the sauce thickens.

7. Serve hot.

## Cook's Note

• Don't worry about the tiny amount of corn flour. There will be so little in each portion as not to worry about and it is important for thickening.

# Courgette Carbonara (V)

- Serves 2-4
- Phase 2

## Ingredients

20g butter

300g smoked bacon

100g button mushrooms

1 shallot or small onion, peeled and chopped

2 cloves garlic, chopped

2 medium courgettes, spiralised

150ml double cream

2 egg yolks

100g Parmesan cheese, grated

Handful of fresh parsley, chopped

Courgette pasta has become really popular in recent years. It makes a great alternative to pasta as it cooks quickly and takes on flavour really well, plus its loaded with fibre and vitamin C.

This sauce is so luxurious with cream, egg and smoked bacon, and it's so quick to make.

I'm so glad I don't count calories because If I did, this recipe would be off the scale! As you will be learning from Zoë, calories are not equal so with that in mind eat away!

## Method

1. Heat the butter in a pan and fry the bacon until crispy then add the mushrooms and cook for 3 minutes in the juices.

2. Add the onion and garlic to the pan and cook for 5 minutes on low heat. Then add the courgette.

3. In a bowl, whisk the cream with the egg yolks and pour into the pan. Turn the heat up and stir through until the cream thickens.

4. Sprinkle the Parmesan over the top and add parsley if you wish.

## Cook's Note

• The Harcombe Diet recommends avoiding smoked bacon (and other smoked foods) if you suffer from Candida. Hopefully you're fine with some in Phase 2, as the smoked bacon really makes this dish.

• Serve with a rocket and tomato salad.

# Sweet Potato and Vegetable Curry (V)

- SERVES **4**
- PHASE **2**

## Ingredients

600g sweet potatoes, peeled and cubed

1 tbsp olive oil

1 onion, peeled and chopped

1 red pepper, deseeded and chopped

4 tbsp of garam masala

1 tsp chilli powder

1 courgette, peeled and chopped

800g chopped tomatoes (2x400g tins will be fine)

400g tin chickpeas, drained

Salt and pepper to taste

This is a lovely vegetarian dish, full of spice. By roasting the sweet potatoes, it helps to hold them together when you add them to the curry.

## Method

1. Preheat the oven to 1705C / 350°F.

2. Drizzle the sweet potatoes with olive oil and a pinch of salt.

3. Roast for 25 minutes or until golden brown/soft.

4. Fry the onion, add the pepper, garam masala, chilli powder, courgette and cook for approximately 5-7 minutes.

5. Add the chopped tomatoes and chickpeas and leave to simmer while the sweet potato cooks.

6. Remove the sweet potatoes from the oven and add them to the pan. Stir them gently into the tomato sauce, so that they don't break up.

7. Season well.

# Wrapped Pork Mince

- SERVES 4
- PHASE 1

## Ingredients

1 green cabbage

150ml boiling water

1 tbsp olive oil

1 red onion, peeled and finely chopped

2 spring onions, finely chopped

2 garlic cloves, finely chopped

1 tsp chilli flakes/ powder

1 tsp ground cumin

1 tsp garam masala

500g pork mince

150g passata

Salt and pepper

This recipe uses cabbage leaves. Green leafy vegetables are the king in terms of plant nutrition and fibre, so it's worth adding them to your daily diet. Cabbage can also be finely chopped and added to salad.

## Method

1. Preheat the oven to 175ºC / 350ºF.

2. Remove the cabbage base and peel off 8 full leaves.

3. Fill a saucepan with boiling water and add the cabbage leaves, leave to simmer for 5 minutes.

4. Fry the olive oil in a separate pan. When the oil is heated, add the onions, garlic, chilli, cumin and garam masala and cook for 5 minutes, stirring.

5. Add the mince and cook until browned.

6. Mix in the passata and add salt and pepper to taste.

7. Spoon 2-3 tbsp of mince mix into the centre of a cabbage leaf and roll up to make a parcel. Place join down into an oven proof dish.

8. Repeat with the remaining cabbage leaves and then bake for 15 minutes.

## Cook's Note

• If you have any mince meat mixture left you can add a tin of chopped tomatoes and serve as a chilli dish.

# Curried Kebabs

- Makes 10 kebabs
- Phase 2
(Can be adapted to phase 1)

## Ingredients

450g meat, diced
(pork, chicken, beef
or a mixture)

4 tbsp olive oil

½ tsp cumin powder

½ tsp cardamom
powder

¼ tsp garam masala

¼ tsp chilli powder

2 cloves garlic,
crushed

1 lemon, halved

1 red and 1 yellow
pepper, deseeded
and chopped

20-30 button
mushrooms (optional)

Barbecue skewers

I'm always thrilled when someone suggests a BBQ, as there are so many real food treats to be had. These kebabs are perfect to take along as your contribution to a BBQ. Plus, it doesn't have to be summer to enjoy these, you can cook them under the grill all year round.

## Method

1. Cut the meat into 2-3cm cubes.

2. Mix the oil, spices and garlic. Squeeze in the lemon juice, ensuring no lemon pips fall into the mixture.

3. Cover the meat with the mixture and marinate for 60-90 minutes.

4. Alternate the pepper with the meat cubes and whole mushrooms as you slide them onto the skewers.

5. Barbecue, or grill under a high flame, for 10 minutes.

## Cook's Note

• Serve with grilled or barbecued aubergine slices or any other barbecued/ grilled vegetables (courgettes work really well too).

• Leave out the mushrooms for a Phase 1 option.

# Baked Meaty Meatballs

- PHASE 2

## Ingredients

500g beef mince

100g liver of your choice (I use chicken)

200g pancetta

1 onion, peeled and chopped

3 cloves garlic, chopped

Handful of fresh basil, finely chopped

2 eggs

2 tbsp olive oil

250ml red wine

1kg passata

1 red pepper, finely chopped

200g Parmesan cheese, grated

I've heard Zoë saying at conferences that she has struggled to find a more nutritious food than liver (even though she doesn't like it!) I think she might like this. Liver is a phenomenal source of vitamin A, B vitamins and a terrific all rounder for minerals from copper to zinc. It's really good to include liver in the family diet, therefore, so that even children get to like this genuine super food from an early age. I sneak liver in to recipes such as Bolognese and stews and my daughter loves them.

## Method

1. Preheat the oven to 175°C / 350°F.

2. Add the raw minced beef, liver and pancetta into the food processor with the onion, garlic, basil and egg and blend everything together.

3. Heat the olive oil in a frying pan.

4. Shape the mixture into meatballs and fry these to seal. Once sealed place in an oven dish.

5. Pour over the red wine, passata, and red pepper. Top with Parmesan and bake for 45 minutes.

# Spanish Stew

## Ingredients

2 tbsp olive oil

1 large onion, peeled and chopped

4 chorizo cooking sausages, sliced

4 chicken breasts, diced

1 courgette, chopped

1 red pepper, deseeded and chopped

1 yellow pepper, deseeded and chopped

3 cloves garlic, chopped

100g of spinach

3 x 400g tins of chopped tomatoes

4 tbsp tomato purée

3 tbsp smoked paprika

2 tbsp chilli powder

2 handfuls of green olives

I love one-pot dishes. This one is quick to put together and would work in a slow cooker too. It's full of Mediterranean flavours, which give a rich tomato sensation. I often bulk cook this recipe and keep portions in the freezer.

## Method

1. Heat the olive oil in a frying pan. Once the oil is hot, add the onion.

2. Add the chorizo sausages and cook them for a couple of minutes to release the spices.

3. Add the chicken breasts and cook for 5 minutes.

4. Once the chicken has browned, add the courgette, peppers, garlic and spinach to the pan.

5. Stir in the chopped tomatoes and tomato purée.

6. Add the chilli powder and paprika, followed by the olives.

7. Leave to simmer without a lid for 30 minutes.

# Stuffed Chilli Peppers

- SERVES 4
- PHASE 2

## Ingredients

200g left over Bolognese (SEE PAGE 87) or chilli beef mixture (SEE PAGE 117)

2 yellow peppers, halved and deseeded

100g cheddar cheese, grated

This recipe is helpful for when you have some left over chilli or Bolognese and wonder what to do with it.

## Method

1. Preheat the oven to 175°C / 350°F.

2. Spoon the left over mixture into the peppers evenly.

3. Sprinkle the peppers with the cheese.

4. Place the peppers on an oven tray and bake for 30 minutes.

# Tuna Steaks and Salsa

## Ingredients

2 limes, juiced

1 garlic clove, chopped

2 tuna steaks

1 red pepper, deseeded and chopped

2 spring onions, chopped

Handful of fresh coriander, chopped

3 tomatoes, chopped

1 fresh chilli, deseeded and chopped

1 tbsp olive oil

1/2 a lime

Fresh tuna steaks are much tastier than the variety found in tins. If you have a fishmonger near you then go and see what they have in stock. This recipe works well with swordfish too.

## Method

1. Marinade the tuna steaks overnight in the juice of 1 lime and garlic.

2. Grill for 5 minutes each side.

3. To make the salsa, mix together the pepper, spring onions, coriander, tomatoes and chilli. Then squeeze in the juice of a lime and a tablespoon of olive oil.

4. Spoon the salsa onto a plate and place the tuna on top with a wedge of lime.

# Meat Feast Pizza

- SERVES 2

- PHASE 2

## Ingredients

2 gammon steaks

2 tbsp tomato puree

1 onion, peeled and chopped

100g cheese, grated

2 tsp mixed herbs

This is truly a meat feast, as the whole base is made from gammon. This is a popular family dinner – loved by men (filling) and children (tasty) alike – and it is so simple to make. I serve mine with purple coleslaw (SEE PAGE 122).

## Method

1. Grill the gammon steak for about 10 minutes each side.

2. Cover the gammon with tomato puree and add the onion on top.

3. Sprinkle the cheese and herbs over the gammon, on top of the onion.

4. Place the gammon back under the grill until the cheese has toasted.

# Hunters Chicken

- SERVES 4
- PHASE 2

## Ingredients

4 chicken breasts

4 rashers smoked bacon

1 x 500g carton of passata

1 tbsp balsamic vinegar

2 heaped tbsp of smoked paprika

3 cloves of garlic, chopped

100g cheddar cheese, grated

So many people ask me for recipes that the whole family will like and this is always a winner. The sauce has a smoky barbeque taste, which is complemented by melted cheese.

## Method

1. Preheat the oven to 175°C / 350°F.

2. Wrap the chicken in the bacon and place into a Pyrex dish.

3. Pour the passata into a large mixing bowl. Add the vinegar and stir.

4. Add the paprika, and garlic and combine.

5. Pour the mixture over the chicken and bacon and sprinkle the cheddar over the meat.

6. Bake in the oven for 30 minutes.

## Cook's Note

- Serve hot with vegetables or salad.

# Stilton and Almond Aubergines (V)

- Serves 2, or 4 as a starter
- Phase 3

## Ingredients

2 aubergines
2 tbsp olive oil
100g stilton
50g flaked almonds

Stilton is so strong in taste that you don't need much to get the flavour. Aubergines are sometimes called the steak of the vegetarian world. The two strong flavours and 'meaty' texture of the aubergines, works really well together. Aubergines generally, like peppers, are natural 'containers' in the vegetable world. We are familiar with stuffed peppers, but we can do far more with aubergine 'boats'.

## Method

1. Preheat the oven to 175°C / 350°F

2. Cut the aubergine lengthways in half and lay face down on a baking tray. Drizzle with the olive oil and roast for 20 minutes.

3. Remove the baking tray from the oven and turn over the aubergines. Mash the flesh of the aubergine with a fork.

4. Crumble the stilton into the aubergine and top with flaked almonds, then place back in the oven for 10 minutes. Serve hot.

## Cook's Note

• Serve on a bed of rocket and sun-dried tomatoes.

• The almonds make this a Phase 3 dish, but it's a tiny mix, so do enjoy this in Phase 2 if you are more of a flexi (as Zoë explains in her books).

# Aubergine Pizza

- Serves 4

- Phase 2

## Ingredients

2 aubergines

2 tbsp olive oil

4 tbsp tomato purée

100g cheddar
cheese, grated

6 rashers of bacon or
250g pancetta, diced

1 onion, peeled and
finely sliced

I prefer this over dough based pizza any day! It's so easy to make and lovely with my purple coleslaw (SEE PAGE 122). Lose weight by eating pizza and coleslaw – yes please!

## Method

1. Preheat the oven to 175°C / 350°F

2. Cut the aubergine lengthways in half and lay face down on a baking tray. Drizzle with the olive oil and roast for 20 minutes.

3. Remove the baking tray from the oven and turn over the aubergines. Mash the flesh of the aubergine with a fork.

4. Cover the flesh side of the aubergine with tomato puree and top with the cheese, bacon and onion.

5. Place back in the oven for 10 minutes to cook through. Serve hot.

# Thai Fish Cakes

- Makes 8 fish cakes

- Phase 1

## Ingredients
### Thai curry paste:

4 tbsp olive oil

One onion, peeled and finely chopped

1 green chilli, deseeded and finely diced

1 inch piece of ginger, peeled and grated

2 cloves garlic, finely chopped

1 stalk of lemon grass, finely chopped

Zest and juice of one lime

1/2 teaspoon salt

## Ingredients
### Fish cakes:

150g skinless salmon

150g prawns

150g skinless cod or other white fish

2 eggs

4 tbsp of Thai curry paste

1 tbsp olive oil

Thai flavours work with fish especially well. The beauty of these fish cakes is that they are not breaded. You can make your own Thai curry paste (with my recipe below) or you can buy one with no sugar/wheat or other unnecessary ingredients.

## Method – Thai curry paste

1. Add all of the ingredients into a food processor or blender and pulse until you have a smooth paste.

## Cook's Note

• You can freeze the paste in ice cube trays. Once set, pop them out of the tray and store in an airtight container in the freezer. Then the cubes can be defrosted at any time to add to a curry or to use as a marinade for fish or meat.

## Method – Fish cakes

1. Add the salmon, prawns and cod to a food processor and blitz.

2. Once blitzed, add the egg and Thai curry paste to the food processor. To bring the mixture together, blitz again.

3. Depending on what size you would like your fishcakes, take a spoonful of the mixture and fry in a small amount of olive oil.

4. Place onto some kitchen towel to absorb any excess oil.

## Cook's Note

• To keep warm, place in the oven on a low heat, maybe while you prepare some Thai vegetables to accompany the fish cakes.

# Chicken Pasanda

## Ingredients

600g chicken breasts

4 tbsp Natural Live Yoghurt

2 tsp ground cumin

4 tsp ground coriander

8 cardamom seeds

2 tsp ground turmeric

1 tsp coconut oil

1 onion, peeled and chopped

1 piece ginger, peeled and chopped

1 green chilli pepper, deseeded and chopped

2 garlic cloves, chopped

200ml chicken stock

50g ground almonds

2 tsp garam masala

1 can unsweetened coconut milk

A curry from scratch beats a takeaway any day and, if you have time, this is really worth the effort. Pasanda curries are mild on the curry Richter scale; you can always spice yours up with extra chilli peppers, but the Pasanda base of coconut and almond flavours are wonderful without overpowering.

## Method

1. Mix the chicken with the yoghurt and spices and leave to marinate while you prepare the rest of the ingredients.

2. Heat the coconut oil in a pan. Once heated, add the onion and cook for about 10 minutes until the onion has softened.

3. Add the ginger, chilli and garlic. Cook for a further 5 minutes until fragrant.

4. Mix the chicken in with the marinade and continue stirring, until the chicken is coloured.

5. When the chicken is cooked through, then add the stock and cover with a lid. Leave to simmer for 30 minutes.

6. Once simmered, add the ground almonds, coconut milk and garam masala and simmer for a further 5 minutes. Serve hot.

## Cook's Note

• Serve with roast cauliflower.

# Cottage Pie with Celeriac and Parsnip Mash

- SERVES 4
- PHASE 2

## Ingredients

2 tbsp olive oil

1 onion, peeled and chopped

500g minced beef

2 tbsp of corn flour

1 carrot, grated

1/2 small swede, peeled and grated

2 beef stock cubes

300ml boiling water

3 parsnips, peeled and chopped

1 celeriac, peeled and chopped

100g butter

100g cheddar cheese, grated

Here is a way to have your pie and eat it! Think of celeriac as your potato replacement, so for roasties, mash, soups and more, it's the perfect swap.

## Method

1. Preheat the oven to 175°C / 350°F.

2. Heat the olive oil in a saucepan. Fry the onion for a couple of minutes; then add the minced beef and fry until brown.

3. Add the corn flour to the beef and stir evenly to coat the meat. Then add the grated carrot and swede.

4. Add the boiling water to a jug and stir in the stock cubes until they melt. Then pour the stock over the mincemeat and stir. The corn flour will help thicken the liquid into a rich gravy.

5. Turn the heat down low and simmer for 30 minutes.

6. While the mixture is simmering, in a separate pan boil the celeriac and parsnips until softened. Once they have softened, add the butter and mash until smooth.

7. Transfer the mixture to a Pyrex dish and cover with the mash and sprinkle with the cheddar. Bake in the oven for 30 minutes.

## Cook's Note

• Don't worry about the tiny amount of corn flour. There will be so little in each portion as not to worry about and it is important for thickening.

# Salmon Fillet and Pea Purée

- SERVES 2
- PHASE 1

## Ingredients

2 salmon fillets

Salt and black pepper for seasoning

200g frozen peas

50g butter

1/2 lemon, juiced

Green vegetables are highly recommended, but peas are higher in carbohydrate than leafy green vegetables, so peas can feel like quite a treat after days of broccoli and kale! For children, peas have natural sweetness, which should be as much as their sensitive taste buds get to experience. This dish is quick to make and the pea Purée has the most amazing colour.

## Method

### For the Salmon

1. Preheat the oven to 175°C / 350°F.

2. Place the salmon fillets onto a baking tray and season well.

3. Place on the middle shelf of the oven and bake for 25 minutes.

### For the Purée

1. Bring a large pan of salted water to the boil and blanch the peas for 3 minutes.

2. Add the peas to a blender along with a little water, butter and lemon juice.

3. Blitz the peas for no more than 2-3 minutes, until a fairly thick, smooth purée has been achieved.

### Cook's Note

• Serve immediately or cool the pea purée as quickly as possible – this will prevent the colour fading.

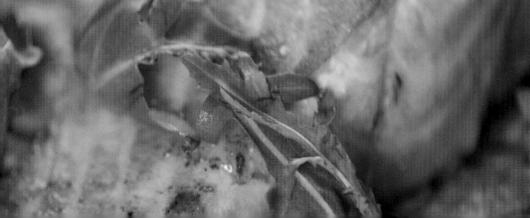

# Garlic Mushroom Chicken

- SERVES 4
- PHASE 2

## Ingredients

2 tbsp of olive oil

1 onion, peeled and finely chopped

6 garlic cloves, finely chopped

2 tbsp corn flour

300ml double cream

Handful of parsley

200g chestnut mushrooms, sliced

4 chicken breasts

150g mozzarella cheese

100g cheddar, grated

This dish is pretty potent and full of garlic – perfect if you've got Candida to attack - plus it tastes great too.

## Method

1. Preheat the oven to 175°C/350°F.

2. Heat the oil in a large non-stick pan.

3. Add the onion and garlic to the pan, then turn the heat down low and leave to sauté for 5 minutes.

4. Add the corn flour to the pan and stir through, making sure it coats the onion. Pour in the double cream and fresh parsley.

5. Mix the mushrooms into the sauce and remove the pan from the heat.

6. Place the chicken breasts into a Pyrex dish and pour over the hot sauce.

7. Break up the mozzarella and place it across the top of the chicken, then sprinkle over the cheddar.

8. Place in the middle shelf of the oven and bake for 35 minutes.

## Cook's Note

• Serve hot with salad or vegetables.

• Don't worry about the tiny amount of corn flour. There will be so little in each portion as not to worry about and it is important for thickening.

# Beef Chilli Pie

- SERVES 4

- PHASE 1 (WITHOUT THE CHEESE) OR PHASE 2 (WITH CHEESE)

## Ingredients

500ml boiling water

1 large celeriac, peeled and cubed

Salt

2 tbsp olive oil

1 onion, peeled and chopped

500g minced beef

1 carrot, grated

2 sticks celery, chopped

1 tbsp dried cumin

1 tbsp garlic powder

1 tbsp chilli powder

1 tbsp smoked paprika

2 x 500g cartons of passata

1/2 tube (75g) tomato purée

3 large handfuls of spinach

100g vintage cheddar cheese, grated

If you like spice, this dish makes a great alternative to cottage pie.

## Method

1. Preheat the oven to 175ºC / 350ºF.

2. Add the celeriac to a pan filled with the boiling water and salt. Boil for 20 minutes until soft.

3. Heat the oil in a large non-stick pan.

4. Add the onion and sauté for a few minutes, then add the beef and cook on a high heat until the meat has browned and started to dry out.

5. Stir in the carrot and celery and add the spices. Then pour in the passata and tomato puree and combine everything together.

6. Place the lid on the pan and simmer for 20 minutes.

7. Add the spinach, which will wilt down quickly and stir through.

8. When the celeriac is ready, mash and season well. Cover the mince mixture with the mash and top with the cheese.

9. Put in the oven and bake for 30 minutes. Serve hot.

# Courgette Fritters (V)

- SERVES 4
- PHASE 3

## Ingredients

2 tbsp olive oil

1 onion, peeled and
finely chopped

450g courgette,
grated

1 tsp salt

2 large eggs

30g Parmesan
cheese, grated

30g cheddar cheese,
grated

1 tsp mixed herbs

60g ground almonds

1/2 tsp baking
powder

## Method

1. Heat the olive oil in a frying pan. Once the oil is heated, add the onion and fry it until brown.

2. Season the courgette with the salt, and leave to soak through for 5 minutes. After 5 minutes, tip the mixture onto a clean tea towel and wring out any excess liquid, then add to the onion.

3. Crack the eggs into the pan and stir well.

4. Add the Parmesan, cheddar cheese, mixed herbs, ground almonds, and baking powder to the mixture and then stir thoroughly.

5. Fry until golden and serve.

## Cook's Note

• Serve with bacon and poached eggs for a super brunch.

• This is a Phase 3 dish because of the almonds. You can always leave out the almonds to add another Phase 2 dish to your menu options.

# Sides

Side dishes can transform plain meat and fish dishes into a completely new eating adventure. Here you'll find a tasty selection that will liven up your dinner.

# Purple Coleslaw (V)

## Ingredients

1 small purple cabbage, finely sliced

1/2 red onion, peeled and finely sliced

2 large carrots, grated

6 tablespoons speedy mayo – (SEE PAGE 124)

## Method

1. In a large mixing bowl add the sliced cabbage, diced onion and grated carrot and mix thoroughly.

2. Pour over the speedy mayonnaise and combine.

3. Store the mayo in an airtight container until ready to serve.

# Moroccan Tagine (V)

- SERVES 6
- PHASE 2 OR 1 (WITH SLIGHT ADJUSTMENT)

## Ingredients

2 large butternut squash, peeled, deseeded and cubed

4 tbsp olive oil

Pinch of salt

2 red peppers, deseeded and chopped

2 aubergines, cubed

1 large red onion, peeled and diced

6 garlic cloves

1 inch piece of ginger, peeled and grated

2 x 400g tinned tomatoes

2 x 500g cartons of passata

2 tbsp cumin

1/2 tsp cinnamon

Handful of fresh coriander, finely chopped

4 fresh apricots, chopped (optional)

This is a great staple side dish, which works equally well with meat, fish or pulses. You can use it as a slow cooker sauce for Moroccan beef or lamb Tagine, by adding diced chunks of either meat.

## Method

1. Preheat the oven to 175°C / 350°F.

2. On one tray, place the butternut squash cubes. Drizzle them with a tablespoon of olive oil and season with salt.

3. On a second tray, add the peppers and aubergine and drizzle with a tablespoon of olive oil. Also season with salt, and then place both trays into the oven.

4. Heat 2 tablespoons of olive oil in a frying pan.

5. Fry the onion and garlic in the frying pan for a few minutes.

6. Stir the ginger into the mixture.

7. While the vegetables are roasting in the oven, add the chopped tomatoes and passata to the frying pan along with the spices and simmer for 20 minutes.

8. When the roasted vegetables are ready, add them to the frying pan and mix everything thoroughly.

9. Stir in the coriander and fresh apricots.

## Cook's Note

• The apricots can be left out for Phase 1, but they will really add to the dish to include them in Phase 2. This can form the base of a fat or carb meal in Phase 2.

# Speedy Mayo (V)

- MAKES APPROXIMATELY
300-350ML
- PHASE 2
(BECAUSE OF THE
VINEGAR)

## Ingredients

275ml light olive oil

2 free range eggs

2 tbsp of lemon juice

2 tbsp cider vinegar

1 tsp salt

The next time you are in a super market, pick up a jar of low-fat mayonnaise and see how many ingredients you don't recognise. You will also find refined oils. Finally, check the sugar content, compared to a full fat mayo, and you will see there is an interesting difference.

When fat is removed, sugar is often added, by now you should know that fat (in our food) is our friend! This recipe is certainly speedy and it uses olive oil and eggs as a base so is really natural. You can customise your mayo by adding fresh garlic, herbs, chilli or mustard for yummy alternatives.

## Method

1. Add all of the ingredients into the plastic jar.

2. Place the stick blender into the jar and then turn it on.

3. Slowly bring the blender up and then back down until you get a thick pale yellow mayonnaise (It takes approximately 30 seconds).

4. Store in an airtight container at the back of the fridge (It will keep for approximately 5 days).

## Cook's Note

• You will need a stick blender and the plastic jar it comes with.

# Roast Cauliflower (V)

## Ingredients

1 head of cauliflower

Pinch of salt

3 tbsp olive or coconut oil

1 tbsp of spices of choice (I use 1 tbsp of garam masala)

I have had my fair share of cauliflower rice but it doesn't quite do it for me. However, roasting cauliflower does. It's crunchy, oily, salty, and yummy – I'm sure you'll love it too!

## Method

1. Preheat oven to 190°C/375°F.

2. Chop up the cauliflower into tiny florets including the stalk (eat that too). Then lay the cauliflower onto a couple of oven trays and sprinkle with oil, salt, and spices.

3. Place into the oven for 25 minutes. Serve warm.

## Cook's Note

• If you are using coconut oil, then you will find it is solid at room temperature. To make coconut oil easier to pour you can soften it by putting the amount needed into a cup and placing the cup into a sink with a couple of inches of hot water.

• Fight over any crunchy bits or eat them before anyone sees!

# Creamed Spinach (V)

## Ingredients

2 tbsp olive oil

50g butter, melted

1 onion, peeled and finely diced

100ml double cream

1/2 tsp nutmeg

200g spinach leaves

Pinch of salt

Pinch of pepper

100g Parmesan cheese, grated

This rich creamy dish takes only minutes to make and will transform a piece of chicken, steak or salmon into a luxurious meal.

Spinach has an extremely high nutritional value - It is a good source of vitamins A, B2, C and K, and also contains magnesium, manganese, folate, iron, calcium and potassium.

## Method

1. Heat the olive oil and butter in a large non-stick pan.

2. Once the oil is heated, add the onion to the pan and stir thoroughly with a wooden spoon.

3. Turn the heat down to the lowest setting and leave the onion to sauté for a few minutes.

4. Pour in the double cream and nutmeg and then bring to the boil.

5. Add in the spinach and then turn down the heat. Place the lid on the pan and leave for a few minutes until the spinach has wilted.

6. Season with salt and pepper and mix thoroughly with a wooden spoon.

7. Top with Parmesan and serve.

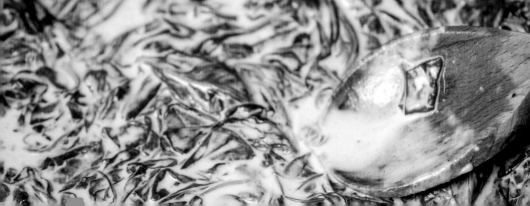

# Celeriac Chips (V)

## Ingredients

1 celeriac, peeled and chopped into chip shapes

Pinch of salt

Water

2 tbsp olive oil

If you are looking for an alternative to potato chips then these are a must. My problem is that I've told so many people about them that when I come to buy a celeriac they have all sold out!

## Method

1. Preheat an oven to 200°C / 400°F.

2. Put the celeriac strips into a pan and cover with water. Season with salt and parboil the celeriac for 10 minutes.

3. Transfer the celeriac strips onto a baking tray, drizzle with olive oil and sprinkle with salt. Roast for 20 minutes.

# Non Bread (V)

## Ingredients

2 eggs

1/2 tsp of dried cumin powder

1/2 tsp mustard seeds

1/2 tsp of baking soda

2 tbsp olive oil

This will give you the feel of a 'nann bread' without the wheat. The baking soda is essential to make the non bread rise.

## Method

1. In a large mixing bowl, whisk the eggs for 5 minutes until fluffy. Then mix in the cumin, mustard seeds and baking soda.

2. Heat the oil in a large frying pan for a few minutes, as you need to get the oil really hot.

3. Pour in the egg mixture and cook for 3 minutes, then flip over to cook the other side.

## Cook's Note

• Serve with salad and curry.

# Butternut Bhaji (V)

- MAKES 8

- PHASE 3

## Ingredients

2 tbsp coconut oil
2 onions, peeled and
finely sliced
1/2 large butternut
squash, peeled,
deseeded and
grated
1 egg
2 tbsp garam masala
2 heaped tbsp
ground almonds
1/2 tsp salt

Traditional bhaji would be gluten-free as they use gram flour (chickpea flour) but many recipes have been adapted and now include wheat flour. This recipe uses grated butternut squash, which gives you a great bhaji texture without the need for any flour. I like to make them when we have a 'curry night'.

## Method

1. Preheat oven to 175°C/350°F.

2. Heat the coconut oil in a large non-stick pan Fry the finely sliced onions and cook on a low heat for 15 minutes until soft and starting to brown

3. Add the grated squash, egg and spices to a mixing bowl. Add the cooked onions, ground almonds and salt and combine. Leave to set for 5 minutes allowing the egg to absorb the almonds

4. Oil a baking tray. Then take a tablespoon of mixture, shape it into your bhaji and place the bhajis onto the tray until the mixture is used up. Season with salt.
Bake for 20 minutes.

## Cooks note

- For extra crispy bhajis you can fry them in some hot oil then and then pat them in kitchen roll before serving, to remove any excess oil.

- These freeze well if you batch cook for the week ahead.

# Puddings

If you are going to cheat – do it in style!

I do love a 'good pud' and when I'm tempted by pretty little things in bakery windows I quickly remind myself of how awful I would feel if I gave in to the temptation.

If you are going to cheat then make it worth your while, make the effort to buy the best ingredients you can afford and spend time putting together something you really enjoy.

I always advise people to have some cheat recipes up their sleeve for entertaining (as most people won't even think they are 'healthy puds'.)

I recently visited the sweetener section of a supermarket and counted over 20 kinds of sugars and sweeteners! Just because the jar may look healthy it's not always the case. Personally I would use Stevia if something needs sweetening, but the more we can deny a sweet tooth, the quicker it disappears.

Even sweeteners' can cause us to release insulin (the fat storing hormone) and bring our cravings back, so these puddings come with a health warning: If you eat too many too often you may gain weight or awaken your Candida cravings so be careful.

Remember Zoë's advice: don't cheat too much; don't cheat too often; be alert and stay in control!

# Gluten-free Pancakes (V)

- SERVES 2 / MAKES 4
SMALL PANCAKES
- PHASE 3

## Ingredients

125g ground almonds

1/4 tsp salt

60ml water

2 eggs

1 tsp olive oil

These can be served as a sweet dish with Greek yoghurt and berries or as a savoury dish, with bacon and scrambled egg.

## Method

1. Mix the ground almonds and salt with the water.

2. Beat the eggs and stir into the mixture until you have a thick batter.

3. Pour the oil into a frying pan and heat until warm.

4. Add two tablespoons of the mixture for one pancake and fry for one minute each side.

# Dark Chocolate Orange and Almond Truffles (V)

- THIS RECIPE MAKES AROUND 40 TRUFFLES, SO DO MAKE THEM WHEN OTHERS ARE AROUND TO SHARE THEM — OR ADJUST THE QUANTITY DOWN ACCORDINGLY — OR FREEZE ANY EXTRAS QUICKLY!

- PHASE 3

I started making truffles as gifts for family when I was in my late teens. I now sell them on a large scale to shops and online! There are so many flavours, but I though I would share a few with you here.

Truffles are a great sweet cheat, as they are so rich that you don't need many.

Usually truffles contain cream, but I wanted to create a version that was dairy-free.

## Ingredients

1 tin organic coconut milk

50g coconut oil

300g 85% dark chocolate, broken into pieces

1 tbsp orange oil

100g toasted flaked almonds

## Method

1. Pour the coconut milk into a pan and add the coconut oil.

2. Take the pan off the heat and add the dark chocolate and orange oil. Allow the mixture to melt the chocolate and stir well.

3. Cover the mixture and leave to set in the fridge.

4. Toast the flaked almonds on a baking tray for 2 minutes.Then leave to one side.

5. Take a teaspoon of the mixture and shape into a ball to make a truffle. Then roll the truffle in toasted flaked almonds.

6. Store in the freezer or fridge.

# Raspberry and Coconut Truffles (V)

- Makes around 40 truffles

- Phase 3

## Ingredients

200g 85% dark chocolate, broken into pieces

100g coconut oil

20g freeze-dried raspberries

50ml unsweetened coconut milk

50g desiccated coconut

50g desiccated coconut (for rolling)

## Method

1. Place a bowl over a pan of simmering hot water, and pour the chocolate and coconut oil into the bowl. Leave over the heat, stirring occasionally with a wooden spoon, until the mixture has melted.

2. Take the pan off the heat and add the freeze-dried raspberries.

3. Add 50g of the desiccated coconut along with the coconut milk and stir until mixed through.

4. Cover the mixture and leave to set in the fridge.

5. Once set, take a teaspoon of the mixture and shape into a ball to make a truffle.Then roll the truffle in the leftover desiccated coconut.

6. Store in the freezer or fridge.

# Egg Yolk Truffles (V)

- MAKES 40
- PHASE 3

## Ingredients

350g 85% dark chocolate, broken into pieces

175g salted butter, cubed

1 tsp vanilla essence

3 egg yolks

Cocoa powder for dusting

Eggs are full of trace minerals, selenium being one of them, which is great for healthy hair, skin and nails. The egg yolk gives such a rich flavour, and without using cream there is more room for more chocolate!

You can flavour anyway you wish, but my favourite by far is sea salt and vanilla and then closely followed by chilli. (For the chilli version, just remove the vanilla and add a teaspoon of ground chilli powder).

## Method

1. Place a bowl over a pan of simmering hot water, and put the chocolate into the bowl. Leave over the heat, stirring occasionally with a wooden spoon, until the mixture has melted.

2. Once the chocolate has melted, remove the bowl from the pan and add the butter and vanilla essence. Stir until you have a thick chocolate sauce.

3. Using a whisk, whisk in the egg yolks and stir the mixture well. The mixture will become thick.

4. Cover the mixture and leave to set in the fridge.

5. Once set, take a teaspoon of the mixture and shape into a ball to make a truffle.Roll the truffle in the cocoa powder.

6. Store in the fridge or freezer.

## Cook's Note

• If you eat them straight from the freezer they last even longer.

# Date and Cashew Nut Fudge (V)

- MAKES APPROXIMATELY
10 BALLS
- PHASE 3

## Ingredients

300g dates
300g cashew nuts
1 tbsp vanilla

This is really high in fruit sugar, but it is a natural alternative to the sticky confectionery option.

## Method

1. Blitz the dates, cashew nuts and vanilla in a food processor.

2. Cover the mixture and leave to set in the fridge.

3. Take a teaspoon of the mixture and shape into a ball.

4. Store in the fridge or freezer.

## Cook's Note

- These taste their best when frozen.

# Apricot and Oat Muesli Bar (V)

- MAKES APPROXIMATELY
10 BARS
- PHASE 3

## Ingredients

250g dried apricots

100g raisins

100g desiccated coconut

100g oats

50g butter, melted

If you want to wean anyone off refined sugar, then recipes like this may help in the short term. They are still high in natural sugar though, so keep them for an occasional cheat. These would make great lunch box snacks for children, however – especially on sports day.

## Method

1. Place the dried apricots, raisins, desiccated coconut, oats and butter in a food processor. Blitz until combined.

2. Transfer the mixture into a tin or lunch box and pat down until flat.

3. Set in the fridge for a few hours.

4. Once set, slice and keep in airtight container in fridge.

# Chocolate Shots (V)

- MAKES 8
- PHASE 3

## Ingredients

300ml double cream

100g 85% dark chocolate, broken into pieces

50g coconut oil (or melted butter)

Flavour of your choice (Brandy, orange, peppermint)

Chocolate desserts can be a good choice when eating out, especially in fancy restaurants, as they usually contain real ingredients such as cream, cocoa powder/very dark chocolate, vanilla and/ or eggs. We use a few of these in this recipe, which works well with orange zest or a teaspoon of peppermint oil added.

## Method

1. Place the double cream into a non-stick saucepan and leave on a low heat to warm through.

2. Add the chocolate pieces to the cream mixture; then stir through.

3. Add the coconut oil (or butter) and any flavour you wish; then stir thoroughly again.

4. Leave to cool before pouring into ramekins or shot glasses. Then set in the fridge for a few hours or overnight.

## Cook's Note

• Will keep well in the fridge for around 4-5 days, or wrap the shots individually in cling film and store standing upright in a Tupperware box in the freezer.

# Hazelnut Spread (V)

- MAKES A LARGE JAR

- PHASE 3

## Ingredients

200g hazelnuts

4 tbsp honey or maple syrup

2 tbsp cocoa powder or cacao

4 tbsp boiling water

Pinch of sea salt

Children love chocolate nut spread, but the best known brand, Nutella(R), was 57% sugar last time I checked. That's really not a great way for our most precious people to start their day. This recipe uses honey or maple syrup – still sugars – but in far smaller amounts. I've made this at my children's cookery school sessions and it went down rather well.

## Method

1. Preheat the oven to 175°C/350°F.

2. Toast the hazelnuts on a baking tray for 3 minutes.

3. Add the hazelnuts, honey/maple syrup, cocoa powder, boiling water and salt to a food processor and blend for 5 minutes.

4. Leave to set in the fridge.

## Cook's Note

• To keep the healthy theme, serve on oat biscuits rather than supermarket bread (which usually has tens of ingredients – many not so nice).

# Squidgy Chocolate Brownie (V)

## Ingredients

225g 70-85% dark chocolate (the darker you go, the richer the brownies), broken into pieces

225g butter, cubed

2 tsp vanilla extract

3 large eggs (beaten)

150g ground almonds

100g toasted flaked almonds

When I need a cake recipe for an occasion, I use ground almonds as my alternative to flour. Almonds are more nutritious than flour, lower in carbohydrate and thus have a much lower impact on the blood sugar level. Almonds also tick the real food box and are therefore naturally satiating. A word of caution for those with a sweet tooth – this is a naturally dark chocolate delight – it tastes rich, rather than sweet, but that's a good thing.

## Method

1. Preheat the oven to 175°C/350°F.

2. Melt the chocolate and butter gently over a low heat in a heavy-based saucepan.

3. Take the pan off the heat, mix in the vanilla and leave to cool.

4. Beat the eggs into the pan along with the ground almonds and flaked almonds.

5. Turn into a 24cm / 9 inch square baking tin, or use a foil one (which can be peeled away from the brownie square to get the 'cake' out more easily).

6. Bake in the oven for 25-30 minutes, by which time the top will have set, but the mixture will still be gooey. Once cooler, cut carefully, four down, four across, into 16 squidgy squares.

# Avocado, Sea Salt and Vanilla Mousse (V)

- SERVES 4
- PHASE 3

## Ingredients

100g 70-85% dark chocolate, broken into pieces.

Pinch sea salt

1 tbsp vanilla essence

50ml almond milk (or cow's milk if you prefer)

2 large ripe avocados, halved and stone removed

This is a wonderful easy recipe, with a dairy-free option. This is so rich that it's best made in shot glasses. If you find it too 'dark' then add a teaspoon of Stevia.

## Method

1. Place a bowl over a pan of simmering hot water, and put the chocolate into the bowl. Leave over the heat, stirring occasionally with a wooden spoon, until the mixture has melted.

2. Whisk the melted chocolate until you have a rich sauce.

3. Stir in the salt and vanilla. Remove from the heat and add the almond milk.

4. Scoop out the avocado flesh into a bowl. Using a fork, mash up the avocado and then add to the chocolate mixture.

5. Whisk the mixture until it is thick (you can also use a food processor or blender if you want an even smoother mixture).

6. Transfer into shot glasses or ramekins and leave to cool.

## Cook's Note

• You can serve this straight away or keep in the fridge for up to 3 days.

# Useful Tables

# Measures and Conversions

All of our recipes are in metric measurements.

Hopefully your scales will measure both metric and imperial but if you like to always work in one version, and convert from the other, here are the conversion tables for you to use. We have used American cup measures here, just in case you always wondered how to convert other recipes you may have into 'normal' measures. The first table is for volume/liquids and the second and third tables are for weight.

Conversion table for volume and liquids:

| USA Cups | Universal Tablespoons | Imperial Fluid oz | Imperial Pints | Metric ml | Other |
|---|---|---|---|---|---|
| 1/16 | 1 | | | 15 | = 3 teasp |
| 1/8 | 2 | 1 | | 30 | |
| ¼ | 4 | 2 | 1/8 | 60 | |
| ½ | 8 | 4 | ¼ | 120 | |
| ¾ | 12 | 6 | 1/6 | 180 | |
| 1 | 16 | 8 | ½ | 240 | |
| 2 | 32 | 16 | 1 | 480 | |
| 4.2 | 68 | 34 | 2.1 | 1000 | = 1 litre |

Conversion table for weight (Imperial to Metric):

| Imperial | Imperial | Metric | Metric |
|---|---|---|---|
| oz | lbs | g | kg |
| 1 | 1/16 | 28 | 0.028 |
| 4 | ¼ | 113 | 0.113 |
| 8 | ½ | 227 | 0.227 |
| 16 | 1 | 454 | 0.454 |

Conversion table for weight (Metric to Imperial):

| Metric | Metric | Imperial | Imperial |
|---|---|---|---|
| g | kg | oz | lbs |
| 100 | 0.1 | 3.5 | 0.22 |
| 250 | 0.25 | 8.75 | 0.55 |
| 500 | 0.5 | 17.5 | 1.1 |
| 1000 | 1 | 35 | 2.2 |

Please note that:

1 teaspoon is approximately 5g of dry weight;

1 dessert spoon is approximately 10g of dry weight; and 1 tablespoon is approximately 15g of dry weight.

Please note that:

1 teaspoon is approximately 5ml of liquid;

1 dessert spoon is approximately 10ml of liquid; and

1 tablespoon is approximately 15ml of liquid.

## Oven Temperature Conversions:

This table is the definitive oven conversion table. All of our recipes list Fahrenheit, centigrade and gas marks to cater for all kitchens. However, this may help you with other recipe books that you may have.

| Fahrenheit | Centigrade | Gas mark | Description |
|---|---|---|---|
| 225 – 275 f | 110 – 135 c | 0 – 1 | Very Cool |
| 300 – 325 f | 150 – 165 c | 2 – 3 | Cool |
| 350 – 375 f | 175 – 190 c | 4 – 5 | Moderate |
| 400 – 425 f | 200 – 220 c | 6 – 7 | Hot |
| 450 – 475 f | 230 – 245 c | 8 – 9 | Very Hot |

## US/UK Food conversions:

This final table is for the different names of foods in the US and UK. We use the UK names in our recipes:

| UK | US | UK | US |
|---|---|---|---|
| Aubergine | Eggplant | Mince | Ground meat |
| Biscuit | Cookie | Muesli | Granola |
| Chips | Fries | Porridge | Oatmeal |
| Coriander (herb) | Cilantro | Prawn | Shrimp |
| Courgette | Zucchini | Rocket (salad) | Arugula |
| Crisps | Chips | Sweets | Candy |

# Recipes

Recipe name: _____

Source: _____

Ingredients

_____
_____
_____
_____
_____
_____

Method

_____
_____
_____
_____
_____
_____
_____

Notes

# Recipes

Recipe name: _____

Source: _____

## Ingredients

_____
_____
_____
_____
_____
_____

## Method

_____
_____
_____
_____
_____
_____
_____

## Notes

# Recipes

Recipe name: _____

Source: _____

## Ingredients

_____
_____
_____
_____
_____
_____

## Method

_____
_____
_____
_____
_____
_____
_____

## Notes

# Recipes

Recipe name: _____

Source: _____

## Ingredients

_____

_____

_____

_____

_____

_____

## Method

_____

_____

_____

_____

_____

_____

_____

## Notes

# For further information

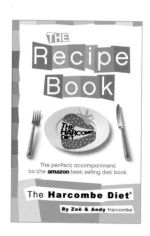

## The Harcombe Diet:
## The Recipe Book

Real food; great taste; optimal health – that's what The Harcombe Diet® is all about and here's how to do it. With over 100 recipes for Phase 1, another 100 for Phase 2 and some seriously special Phase 3 cheats, this is the ultimate diet-recipe book. If you want to eat well, lose weight and gain health – this is a must for your kitchen shelf.

ISBN 978-1-907797-07-1

## The Harcombe Diet
## Phase 1 Recipe Book

This book makes Phase 1 of The Harcombe Diet easy and enjoyable with over 100 real food recipes – all sugar-free, nut-free, gluten-free and mainly low-carb. Oatmeal smoothie... Salmon Provençal... Homemade beef burgers... Spicy chicken... Cajun ham... Carrot & ginger soup... Curried coleslaw... If any of these appeal to you, you'll love this simple, no-fuss recipe book.

ISBN 978-1-907797-68-2

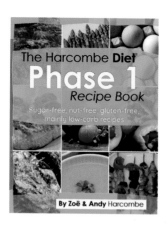

# Index

Roasted Chickpeas 54

Roasted Nuts 40

Soda Bread 28

Speedy Mayo 124

Spiced Butternut Squash and
    Coconut Soup 66

Spiced Parsnip and Apple Soup 70

Squidgy Chocolate Brownie 144

Stilton and Almond Aubergines 106

Stuffed Goats Cheese Peppers 44

Super Smoothie 33

Sweet Potato and Vegetable Curry 92

## W

Wrapped Pork Mince  93